UTOPIA NOWHERE

BY

SOLANGE HERTZ

TUMBLAR HOUSE
ARCADIA
MMXII

ISBN 978-0-9842365-9-6

Utopia Nowhere
© 2012 by Solange Hertz

"There has been maturing in the wishes and expectations of all the seditious members of society the advent of a *certain universal republic* which should be founded on the absolute equality of men and on community of goods, and in which there should no longer be national distinction, nor should any recognition be given to the authority of the father over his sons, nor of public power over the citizens, nor of God over men united in civil commonwealth. All of which things, should they become actual, would cause tremendous social convulsion, such as is now being experienced and felt ..."

Pope Benedict XV Moto Proprio *Bonum et sane* July 25, 1920

Table of Contents

TO BEGIN WITH ...

Adam was a great disappointment to the devil. His wife had been easily deceived by his wiles, and when Adam followed her into disobedience against his better judgment, the angelic father of lies must have felt certain that all material creation was within his grasp. With Adam in his power, everything over which Adam had been given dominion would naturally fall under his exquisite satanic control, to rearrange and govern as he saw fit.

As Perfecter and Re-creator of the Universe, Satan would build on earth the Utopia he had failed to establish on high. His savage thirst for empire would be slaked, for naturally he expected that Adam, with the shamefaced Eve at his side, would become his terrestrial ally in the Great Revolution he had started in heaven. But this never happened.

Unlike Eve, Adam "was not deceived" (*1 Tim. 2:14*). First he hid, then he blamed his wife, but in the end our good father repented. Because even in his fallen state he was still head of the human family, he earned a second chance not only for himself, but for all of us. To the devil's horror, instead of persisting in their disobedience, our first parents humbly accepted the punishments God meted out to them.

Let this be a lesson to us, for they ended by setting a good example. Determined to remain subject to God's rule as best they could, they incurred, of course, the Adversary's undying enmity. This brought on the state of affairs now generally known as "the human condition," and under the circumstances, we are very fortunate to be in it.

But the devil remained steadfast in his desire to supplant the divine economy with his own artificial government, and he has been able to whip up plenty of enthusiasm for his program among Adam's descendants. Beginning with Adam's firstborn Cain, many would be led to "make the world a better place" by concocting utopias to inflict on themselves and others.

As the ages rolled on, humanity inevitably polarized around those two contingents designated in *Genesis* as "the seed of the woman" and "the seed of the serpent." One wanted no more nonsense, because obviously the situation was bad enough, and the other was sure it could solve everything if only God were kept out of it. St. Augustine saw these irreconcilable factions as the City of God and the City of Man. Both are world governments in the largest possible sense, and they are locked in mortal combat till the end of time, for nothing less than the souls of men.

When "separation of Church and state" was established as a political principle in modern times, the two Cities began parting company visibly before the eyes of all, but only to square off properly and get at each other better. Like any couple whom God has joined together, Church and state can never be divorced. No matter how many fictitious decrees are handed down by the court of domestic relations, they are still married. And that precisely, is what causes all the trouble.

The text which follows deals with this touchy subject. Some minor redundancies may be found in it, for it is adapted from articles which appeared in the United States in *The Remnant*, in Scotland in *Apropos*, in England in *Christian Order*, and in France in *Action Familiale et Scolaire*. Three chapters, "The Usan Catholic" and those dealing with Joan of Arc and devotion to the Sacred Heart of our Lord, were originally delivered as talks at the annual Christ the King Symposium sponsored by the Christian Law Institute in El Paso, Texas. All focus on Utopia, that mysterious social aberration which always threatens, but never comes to fruition, because the very word means *Nowhere*.

Solange Hertz
Big Rock, Leesburg, Virginia
Feast of the Purification
February 2,1993

CONSPIRACY

In his well known political novel *Coningsby*, Benjamin Disraeli said of world government:

> *All great events have been distorted, most of the important causes concealed, some of the principal characters never appear, and all who figure are so misunderstood and misrepresented that the result is a complete mystification.*

Serious supporters of the conspiracy theory of history can expect to be relegated without compunction to the lunatic fringe by professional historians, of all people in a position to know better. Even in the public mind, sensitivity to conspiracy is dangerously close to paranoia. The very word conspiracy has become synonymous with plotting. Our dictionary bears this out, where the primary definition is given as "an evil, unlawful, treacherous or surreptitious plan formulated in secret by two or more persons; plot."

Aha! This conjures up a familiar scenario of sinister bushy-browed characters with high I.Q.'s and aquiline noses, hunched around a table in the dark of night (in a dank basement or a luxurious hideaway as the case may be) masterminding a world takeover. Operating as the head of an octopus with tentacles conveying secret directives to subsidiary plotters in every corner of the globe, they are able to manipulate public opinion, pulverize opposition, create crises. Anyone capable of furthering their nefarious plans may find himself catapulted overnight into a position of influence.

Such a view of conspiracy is indeed ridiculous. Although to some extent such machinations have been concocted here and there throughout history, an operation manifesting the cosmic intensity, historical continuity, extension, coordination and intelligence of the one deploying in our day defies human explanation. Probably the readiest clue to what is taking place lies in the original meaning of the word conspiracy, easily found in any Latin dictionary. There *conspiratio* is defined as "unison, harmony, agreement, union," derived from the word's basic meaning, which is simply "breathing together."

Although Cicero attributed malevolent conspiracy to Catiline, and Julius Caesar to certain military antagonists, the word itself was far from pejorative. Mostly it conveyed a happy consensus of *"omnium bonorum"* on the part of gaggles of like-minded buddies. Alas, this benign definition now figures last in the English dictionary, which does allow that the old "breathing together" might possibly mean no more than a "combination in bringing about a given result," but presents such a meaning as unusual. History has given conspiracy a very bad name.

Good or bad, however, conspiracy is inseparable from God's creation. Whoever doesn't believe that conspiracy is an active ingredient of history quite simply does not believe in the existence of the devil. Worse still, perhaps he doubts the existence of God, who revealed to us in both the Old and the New Testaments that mankind's otherwise inexplicable ills are the work of the author of evil: "An enemy has done this!" (*Matt. 13:28*). As we might expect, first among those deriding the notion of a malevolent conspiracy are the devil himself and his fellow conspirators, laboring as they do to persuade us they don't exist, so as to conspire more efficiently.

The less the plotters know about the source of their inspiration the better. Multitudes of human beings whom sin has enslaved to Satan do his work thinking it is their own idea. They are no less conspirators, however, for they "breathe together" the common impious breath which animates them as a single body to further the infernal cause. Wittingly or unwittingly, harnessed individually by their particular vices and appetites, they act as one to promote that cause. When the conspiracy first crested visibly in the eighteenth century, Voltaire reduced all their strivings to two words, *"Ecrasez l'infâme!"* "Crush the unspeakable thing!" which is, of course, none other than the Mystical Body of our Lord and Savior Jesus Christ.

So far only one modern historian has dealt with the devil as an integral part of history, unmasking him as the source of the plot. That historian is the Mother of God, divinely appointed destroyer of all heresies, who at Fatima in 1917 and later, pointed out to Sr. Lucy the true drift of events. She had already done so to Mélanie Calvat at La Salette in 1846, following on her revelations to St. Catherine Labouré a generation previously. Two centuries before these, in the autobiography she dictated to the Spanish nun Venerable Maria de Agreda, she had described in several places the great councils called by Satan in hell to plan the strategy best suited to destroy the eternal kingdom visibly begun by God on earth.

Whoever thinks history "just happens," needs to read *The Mystical City of God* for proper perspective: Called on for their opinions after the Crucifixion, the higher ranking demons agreed that it would be impossible to reverse the Redemption now accomplished by Christ, but they could labor to prevent the application of its fruits. They advised that, "In accordance with the new order of assistance and favor established by God for the salvation of men, they should seek new ways of hindering and preventing the work of God by deceits and temptations so much the greater."

To this end the demons "spent nearly a full year after the death of Christ in conferring and considering among themselves the state of the world." Redistributing their spheres of work, "they resolved to continue to propagate idolatry in the world," and "Wherever idolatry would fail, they concluded to establish sects and heresies, for which they would select the most perverse and depraved of the human race as leaders and teachers of error." Our Lady tells us that Lucifer approved this counsel, whose effects are so evident in the world today. Anyone still unconvinced of the reality of the satanic conspiracy through all the evil he sees around him, should be convinced, says she, "by the vast and powerful remedies and helps which the Savior thought it necessary to leave behind in His Church. For He would not have provided such antidotes if our ailment and danger of eternal death were not so great and formidable!"

+

In his fury against the infant Church Satan sought particularly the cooperation of:

> *... the scribes and Pharisees and all of the Jews, whom he perceived still clinging to their obstinate perfidy. He betook himself to them and by many suggestions filled them with envy and hatred against the Apostles and the faithful of the Church; thus, through the unbelievers he roused persecution, which he could not begin himself.*

Saul of Tarsus had been the conspiracy's first ready instrument among the Jews, and after his conversion, according to Agreda, hell decided to continue using unreconstructed Judaism as their spearhead of choice in the work of destruction so effectively begun: "Let us raise a general persecution against the faithful, for we have at our service the whole of Judaism !"

By virtue of its obsessive craving for a temporal messianic kingdom of its own in this world, Judaism throughout history has proved only too easy to harness. Gougenot des Mousseaux, a French Catholic scholar highly esteemed by Pope Pius IX, wrote over a hundred years ago in *Le Juif*:

> *Anti-religious forces, especially the anti-Christian ones which characterize this day and age, exhibit a concentration and universality bearing the seal of the Jew. He is the supreme promoter of the unification of peoples because he is cosmopolitan par excellence; by giving license to freethinking, he prepares the way for what he calls messianic times, in other words, for the days of his universal triumph. He attributes their imminent realization to the principles circulated by the 18th century philosophers, men who were both unbelievers and kabbalists, who laid the groundwork for the judaization of the world.*

In view of what St. Paul first perpetrated against the Christians in his misguided zeal, and what he eventually suffered as a consequence of hell's policy, no one was better qualified than he to formulate the Church's first formal recognition of the conspiracy theory. He wrote to the Ephesians from prison in Rome, "Our wrestling is not against flesh and blood; but against principalities and powers, and against the rulers of this world of this darkness, against the spirits of wickedness in the high places" (*Eph. 6:12*). To reject the conspiracy theory of history out of hand in the face of such testimonials would appear to be temerarious at the very least.

Long before St. Paul, God told the prophet Jeremias, "A conspiracy is found among the men of Juda, and among the inhabitants of Jerusalem" (*Jer.11:9*). Both scripture and tradition tell us that, beginning with Adam and Eve in Eden, a fallen angelic intelligence working through human agents is orchestrating a plan to displace God in His own creation. All the while lending indispensable support, mere human beings on their own could never have conceived so monstrous a rebellion flying in the very face of reality, let alone have provided the necessary force and continuity to implement it. Sinful men's lives are too short, their wills too weak, their thinking too limited. Bound to bodies shackled by recurring hunger and fatigue, they are incapable of an effort which must be sustained at white heat literally through centuries.

Henry Ford said history is bunk. Napoleon called it "a collection of lies statesmen have agreed upon." With the sophisticated technology now set in place, the father of lies can and does rewrite history to suit his own purposes. After all, he invented "disinformation" in Eden and has had centuries to perfect the technique. Written history by now is little more than a highly developed form of fiction, lately sharing the world scene with that other fiction known as "scientific truth." Neither is concerned with substantial reality, but only with what proves useful for the moment. For generations already, history is what happens in the history books. Education rests on texts revised with every shift in public policy. Earthshaking events having little or no basis in fact can now be media-manufactured almost out of whole cloth.

As seemingly unrelated happenings unwind themselves in the daily papers and on TV, only faith discerns the dim outlines of the mortal battle between good and evil that is going on among nations as among individuals. Far from being a mindless dialectic of conflicting interests, history is the record of an apocalyptic struggle between those two primordial kingdoms - that of God and that of the devil. Our Lord warned His disciples that they would be subject to the same kind of attack as He. Regarding their antagonists, He makes it clear that, "If I had not come, and spoken to them, they would not have sin; but now they have no excuse for their sin" (*John 15:22*). Try as it will to ignore Him, human society does so at its peril.

After Christ entered history and assumed His throne at the right hand of the Father, history was endowed with a completely new dimension. In Him, divinity and humanity had been wed forever in an indissoluble union. History which does not take into account its new metaphysical dynamism is indeed bunk, where incoherent" facts" lend themselves to any kind of interpretation. Faith alone assesses them properly. As Donoso Cortes so aptly put it, "Theology is the light of history." This is why, to deal with conspiracy, St. Paul didn't tell the Ephesians to perfect their espionage. He told them to "take up the shield of faith," and to "put on the armor of God, that you may be able to withstand the deceits of the devil" (*Eph. 6:6,11*), who has given conspiracy the bad name it now labors under.

+

Conspiracy was not the devil's invention. It is true an occult, highly organized force for evil does exist, mounted by him with deadly effectiveness, but had there not been another conspiracy which predated his, he could never have thought of it. The devil is not "original." Like everyone else, he was created. Whatever he does he copies. His conspiracy is therefore more properly called an anti-conspiracy, mirror image of a real one. God is the author of conspiracy. Rooted like everything else in natural law, it ultimately derives from that ineffable cooperation of divine persons in the Most Holy Trinity, where the Father and the Son act as one in the bond of the Holy Ghost.

Through the mediation of the Son made man, the trinitarian cooperations have been projected into, nay, actually joined with those of mankind. A mystical transubstantiation of human society, as it were, not only became possible, but actually began. Human society would be changed, not in its form, which remains the same, but in its substance. This plan of heaven's to take over the world by supernaturalizing its inhabitants may properly be called the Holy Ghost's Conspiracy. Like the devil's, it is something only faith can explain. Unlike the devil's, however, it will succeed, and it will have no end.

It began with natural creation, when as yet "the earth was void and empty, and darkness was upon the face of the deep," when "the spirit of God moved over the waters." (*Gen. 1:2*). This life giving breath of the Father and the Son, which produced everything that exists, has never ceased its divine action and is at work even now. The first natural creation in the beginning was merely a foundation for the transcendent supernatural creation which was to follow and is still in progress. The Psalmist, foreseeing the "mighty wind coming" which would reach a climax with the birth of the Church at the first Pentecost, uttered in prophecy the verse she would pray ever after, all over the world, for the commemoration of this feast:

Emitte Spiritum tuum et creabuntur, et renovabis faciem terrae! "Send forth thy spirit, and they shall be created: and thou shalt renew the face of the earth!" (*Ps. 103:30*).

Scripture tells us the promised renewal began in Jerusalem, only ten days after our Lord's Ascension, when the sound of a gale blowing from heaven "filled the whole house." Dispatching this mighty gust to the earth was our Lord's first official exercise of the royal power He assumed when He mounted His throne in heaven. The Vulgate calls it a *spiritus vehemens*, a spiration so violent and fiery, that all who breathed it began prophesying on the spot, being "filled with the Holy Ghost." And with that the Christian Conspiracy was underway.

Under the headship of St. Peter, God's one, holy, universal and apostolically stable world government was inaugurated on earth. It is indefectible and will continue eternally, for it is the Church. The satanic forces have every reason to tremble before its advance, for the business of the Church is not confined to piety in the private sector. Nor is it exclusively spiritual. It threatens the princedom of this world with dissolution down to its roots, materially, visibly, really, politically. As Soloviev so happily pointed out in *The Universal Church*:

> *The Church is not only the perfect union of mankind with God in Christ, but it is also the social order established by the Divine Will in which and through which this union of the divine and the human may be accomplished...*
>
> *Man's social existence upon earth cannot be excluded from the new union of the human and the divine which is accomplished in Christ. If the elements even of our material life are transformed and sanctified in the sacraments, how can the social and political order, which is an essential form of human existence, be left a prey to the warfare of selfish ambitions, the clash of murderous passions and the conflict of erroneous opinions? Since man is essentially a social being, the ultimate aim of the working of God in mankind is the creation of a perfect universal society.*

From the outset those chosen to inaugurate this renovation exhibited some characteristics commonly associated with conspiracy. Gathered secretly "all together in one place," they were few in number to begin with, in this case hardly 120. In other words, they were the proverbial dedicated "active minority" it always takes to initiate any significant change in the world. (It's notorious that majorities can rarely be depended on for starting anything constructive.) Articulate and persuasive, they baptized 3000 listeners on their first day of operation. Fluent in "divers tongues, according as the Holy Ghost gave them to speak," for them the punishment of Babel was suspended. The language they spoke, anyone could understand. (*Acts 1-2* passim).

As in all conspiracies, the overall strategy is developed at the summit and need never concern the rank and file. Theirs would come from the highest possible source, for they had been promised that "The Holy Ghost... will teach you all things, and bring all things to your mind" (*John 14:26*) relevant to whatever duties the conspirators might be called upon to discharge. The divine leader makes his directives known through a communications system impenetrable to the enemy, who for all his spiritual powers, has no access to the supernatural. He "perceiveth not these things that are of the Spirit of God, for it is foolishness to him and he cannot understand" (*1Cor. 2:14*).

Our Lord told the Christian confederacy they would be furthermore "endued with power from on high" (*Luke 24:49*). Once committed to the cause, they need only exercise their diverse talents in the very same Spirit who conferred them in order to achieve their objectives: "Now there are diversities of graces, but the same Spirit; And there are diversities of ministries, but the same Lord; And there are diversities of operations, but the same God, who worketh all in all" (*1 Cor. 12:4-6*). Being the bond of Christians as He is the Bond of the Blessed Trinity, the Holy Spirit inspires the entire Conspiracy as proper protagonist and mastermind. He is its very Breath, their *Esprit de corps*. Him the conspirators truly "breathe together," conspiring with the trinitarian Persons towards the common goal under the guaranteed headship of Peter.

+

Knowing that "whosoever are led by the spirit of God, they are the sons of God" (*Rom. 8:14*), the devil likewise seeks adoptive progeny among those allowing themselves to be led by his inspirations into conspiring with his breath. Today the Holy Ghost's

Conspiracy seems actually to be withering under his assaults, some of its key positions occupied by hell's henchmen. Obviously the trouble cannot lie with the high command in heaven and must be looked for in the lower echelons. There, as with all conspiracies, the causes of recreance are pretty much always the same: breakdowns in communication, relaxation of discipline, supply failures or outright insubordination and defection. Supernaturally, these translate easily enough into insufficient prayer and mortification, neglect of Mass and the Sacraments, and flouting the commandments and counsels of God or His Church.

Deficiencies in any of these areas are sufficient to explain corporate loss of morale, social failures ultimately resting as they do on those of individuals. There can be no conversion of society where men do not conform their wills to God's. The Mother of God told Mary of Agreda:

> *Innumerable are the souls I have saved from the infernal dragon because of their devotion to me, even though they recited only one Ave, or said only one word in my honor and invocation... But sinners and reprobates do no such thing; because the wounds of sin, not being of the body, do not distress them, and the oftener they are committed, the less regret or sorrow do they cause. The second sin is already like wounding a dead body which knows neither fear, nor defense, nor sensation.*

Last to blame is the devil. Laboring in the infernal councils to perfect his anti-conspiracy modeled on God's, he is forced to attempt a universal government of his own. For our sins, he began dismantling Christendom by inspiring the creation of man-made democracies politically independent of the Church and all supernatural order. These were followed by socialist regimes built on atheism as principle. Now it would seem that by preaching freedom to the victim peoples, he is beginning to realign them into the global kingdom of this world foretold by St. John in the Apocalypse.

When the luciferian conspiracy reaches its culmination, says the Apostle, Satan will command adoration of the beast "whose wound to death was healed" - believed by most exegetes to be resurrected paganism. In what appears to be a parody of the action of the Holy Ghost, the devil will even be allowed "to give life to the image of the beast, and that the image of the beast should speak" (*Apo. 13:15*). What is merely natural will be made to appear supernatural, and the deception will draw multitudes into its toils.

At best the conspiracy theory of history shows us what is really going on "through a glass, in a dark manner" (*1 Cor. 13:12*), for real history, like biography, must begin at the end, and the universal judgment is not yet. As Fr. Arminjon put it in *The End of the Present World* - a work highly esteemed by the Little Flower and her family:

> *In the brightness of God's light will be seen clearly and in detail all crimes public and secret which were perpetrated in every place and at all times. The life of each human subject will be completely unfolded. No circumstance will be omitted; there will be not one action, one word, not one desire which will not be made known... The judgment will untangle and pull out all the twisting threads of those cleverly woven intrigues.*
>
> *It will show in their true light those base retractions and cowardly connivances which men invested with public power sought to justify, either by invoking the specious excuse of reasons of state or by covering them with the mask of piety or disinterest.*

Individual casualties may be very heavy, with all their chaotic consequences, but as they say in India, one tree falling makes more noise than a forest growing. Failures serve only to clear the way for the living wood. Amid the din of crashes, the Holy Ghost's Christian Conspiracy pursues its eternal work. Without Him who established the very heavens "by the breath of his mouth" (*Ps.32:6*), no organized endeavor comes to fruition. With Him, no endeavor can fail.

Propelled by that gentle zephyr with hurricane force we call the Spirit of God, the Conspiracy spread over the earth like wildfire as soon as it was loosed among men. Beginning with the Roman Empire, it effected exactly what conspiracies are supposed to effect: a world takeover. Transforming every obstacle in its path, it eventually left Byzantium to its errors and established in the west upon the Rock of Peter that incomparable new world order known as Christendom. As an empire it was not perfect, but it disseminated the seeds of the divine Conspiracy everywhere, even discovering on its way another whole hemisphere in America for future operations.

At that first Pentecost "the multitude of believers had but one heart and one soul" (*Acts. 4:32*), who drew the divine breath in common, and despite all appearances to the contrary, they still do. Inevitably the universal kingdom under Christ the King for which their conspiracy was forged will succeed. They can be certain of this, for God promised it to His Mother. Before the King was born she was told:"He shall be great and shall be called the Son of the most High; and the Lord God shall give him the throne of David his father; and he shall reign in the house of Jacob forever. And of his kingdom there shall be no end" (*Luke 1:32-3*).

All the devil has is time, and time is not eternal. It's only a matter of time before the Holy City delineated in the Apocalypse becomes a reality: "Having the light of God," this divine utopia:

> *...hath no need of the sun, nor of the moon, to shine in it. For the glory of God hath enlightened it, and the Lamb is the light thereof. And the nations shall walk in the light of it: and the kings of the earth shall bring their glory and honor into it. And the gates thereof shall not be shut by day, for there shall be no night there. And they shall bring the glory and honor of the nations into it. There shall not enter into it any thing defiled, or that worketh abomination or maketh a lie, but they that are written in the book of life of the Lamb" (Apo.21:11,23-27).*

Satan, poor devil, gets all the others.

CAIN'S PAIN

The specter of world union without benefit of clergy - seen lurking in the shadows ever since the Renaissance by anyone who knew where to look - is suddenly taking on flesh. Striding ever more confidently through the current scene, it is now taking on the role scripted for it at the outbreak of the so-called First World War. At that time the most obvious clue to the specter's ominous presence lay in the fact that this strangely concocted conflict was soon, by near common consent, referred to as a world war.

And it was the first. Regardless of the number of participants, no war had ever been so designated, not even by Nebuchadnezzar, Alexander the Great, Napoleon or any other conqueror who fancied the global arena. Apparently animated by a simple straightforward desire to concentrate power in their own hands, their naked objective was no more complicated than domination of weaker nations. They were, furthermore, content to accomplish this under the aegis of whatever gods were adored at the time. Our First World War, however, to hear the victors tell it, was not waged to satisfy any lust for power, either individual or collective. It was a crusade. Its announced purpose, for which hitherto unheard of numbers of human lives were sacrificed, was for the benefit of all mankind - to make the world safe for democracy!

Indeed, to ensure the implementation of this novel objective, it was found necessary to establish a supranational world authority into the very terms laid down in the peace treaty. "In order to promote international cooperation and to secure international peace and security," the signatories set up a League of Nations with a World Court, binding their respective governments to settle future differences henceforth in Geneva. As might be expected, the promoter of this provision was Woodrow Wilson, the President of the United States, the one nation of the world which had been put to ether on purely secular principles to begin with. Ironically enough, it was the U.S. Senate which refused to ratify this particular point, American public opinion being then unready to take so drastic a step in that direction.

Benedict XV saw only too clearly what that direction was. On July 25, 1920, only a few months after the Armistice, he issued a

Motu Proprio for the celebration of the fiftieth anniversary of the proclamation of St. Joseph as Patron of the Universal Church, wherein he called attention to "a cause of disturbance ... which has crept into the very heart of society." He found it no coincidence that, "The scourge of war descended on the human race just at that moment when it had become deeply affected with naturalism." Needless to say, God's. name was not destined to figure either in the Versailles Treaty or the Covenant of the League.

The Pope warns:

> *There has been maturing in the wishes and expectations of all the seditious members of society the advent of a certain universal republic, which should be founded on the absolute equality of men and on community of goods, and in which there should no longer be national distinction, nor should any recognition be given to the authority of the father over his sons, nor of public power over the citizens, nor of God over men united in civil commonwealth. All of which are things, which, should they become actual, would cause tremendous social convulsion, such as is now being experienced and felt by not a small part of Europe.*

With a hindsight of seventy years, it is easy to assess the truth of this prediction.

Only where there is radical separation of Church and state, formal political cleavage between the natural order and the divine to the disregard of the latter, can man envisage this particular kind of world unity. Given the constitution of God's Creation, such a concept lies outside reality. It is, in other words, insane. Speaking of the "contagion of socialism, than which nothing is more opposed to Christian wisdom," Benedict XV reinforced his words with those of Leo XIII, who also warned that "both justice and reason forbid the destruction of that order which Divine Providence has ordained."

Although it proved to be an irreversible beginning, the League enjoyed a very limited success. Certainly it was powerless to prevent the Second World War, which the Mother of God had predicted at Fatima a year before the carnage of the First was suspended. Actually a continuation of the first, this second war is still in progress in diverse guises. Undergoing successive "hot" and "cold" phases, it bids fair to prolong itself into the Third World War which our Lady also promised us unless some very special demands from heaven are met.

With the surcease of this second conflict, those "seditious members of society" of which Benedict XV spoke were nothing daunted. Animated by what they now saw as pressing necessity, they set up the United Nations Organization to replace the old League. This time the headquarters were located in the United States, which by now had seen the light and bound itself officially to contribute both financially and ideologically to the acclaimed salvation of the future.

In 1965 even the reigning Pope appeared to have been converted. Paul VI crossed the Atlantic to address its solemn assembly and proclaimed its deliberations "the last hope of the world." Like that of Caiphas of old, his divinely instituted office may have led him unwittingly to utter prophecy, for as the Parousia God ordained approaches apace, the government offered by the UN may indeed be the last hope for this world for which our Lord told us He "does not pray" (*John 17:9*). Quite evidently it offers little hope for Christianity.

+

To understand the source and nature of secular globalism, it is useless to analyze the strategies employed by its elitists in their determination to make the world safer and safer for democracy. Nor is it necessary to waste time exposing political feints and scams like *glasnost* and *perestroika*, which have lately heralded the Soviet Union's sudden conversion to "democracy." All the while crying for freedom from oppression, the world seems actually to be at grips with epidemic insecurity. A psychologist acquainted with history might conclude that what Europe is really yearning for is the security of its old mother's womb: the Roman Empire. Nor would he be surprised to find this yearning most acute, albeit unsuspected, among those outcasts which never formed part of it: the United States, the Scandinavian countries and Soviet Russia, which are among the most avid for "world government."

Obviously, the explanation for convulsions of such magnitude as we witness today can be found only in the spiritual order. It is sufficient to cast the eyes of faith on the opening chapters of *Genesis* to see that "globalism" was one of the earliest effects of original sin, a perversion of that divinely implanted instinct for unity which came with man's creation to the image and likeness of his Creator. Whether he will or no, it modifies his whole human comportment: His God is a Unity of Persons, and so must man be, and all his kind, who are patterned on the Deity.

Outside this unity, no like persons can exist. Whether he will or no, man is constitutionally programmed for togetherness, both in body and in soul. Whenever man becomes separated from God or from other men, his urge for unity does not disappear, for it is intrinsic to his being; it only increases through frustration. We have God's word for the fact that "it is not good for man to be alone!" (*Gen. 2:18*). Like the inability to love experienced by the damned, the desire for unity here below is felt as an intolerable hunger which cannot be satiated. Is it any wonder that today, separated from God politically and morally as never before, man is becoming mad with desire for unity in this world, which now offers the only future he can believe in? Even the Holy Sacrifice of the Mass has been affected, now distorted into a "celebration of community!"

Scripture tells us that after the murder of Abel, Cain fell under a curse which rendered the earth unproductive to his cultivation. Worse yet, he became" a fugitive and a vagabond." Fleeing God's presence, he "dwelt as a fugitive" to the east of Eden with his wife, by whom he sired a race of outcasts like himself (*Gen. 4:11-16*). Separated from God and from his father's family, abhorred by them, he is protected from their vengeance only by a mysterious mark God set upon him. In his anguish he tries to make a place for himself, to provide himself and his clan with some semblance of community. We are told, "He built a city." This was a substitute of his own making, artificial, but quite understandable under the circumstances. There was certainly nothing wrong in building a city. It was probably a good idea.

What was not a good idea is what followed, for Cain "called the name thereof by the name of his son" (*Gen. 4:17*). Having repudiated his ancestry and all that went with it, the guilt-ridden Cain soon found it hard to live in the present, for it had become unbearable to him: "My iniquity is greater than that I may deserve pardon" (*Gen. 4:13*). He would therefore live in a world to come, of his own building, planned to relieve his special pain. So he named his new city after his son, fruit of his own loins. The son was Henoch, whose name probably means "initiation," or "dedication," for he was Cain's new beginning. (He is not to be confused with that later Henoch who "walked with God.") The secular city, a social unit with no reference to anything beyond itself, dates from this moment. It was born of angst, alienation and a desire for self-sufficiency. It was an alternative to utter despair.

Obviously Cain was not a traditionalist. In today's think-tank parlance he would be called a futurist. He would forget the past and bend all his efforts to "leaving the world a better place." In this endeavor he would place all his hope of immortality, even if there was no possibility of his ever seeing its realization. Material progress would be his ideal, his new religion. When he named the city after his son, he prefigured all those who would repudiate the Fourth Commandment, on which all true tradition rests. After the devil, Cain is the father of revolutionaries.

His futurism is widely accepted today by the misguided, who see it not as the virulent heresy it is, but as a virtue, a special form of altruism. A young Catholic father was overheard informing his mother not long ago that he owed her absolutely nothing, because his duties henceforth were to his children. This seems to be the new law of Corban for our secular age. In His own day Our Lord condemned its misapplication on the part of hypocrites who neglected their parents under cover of making donations to religion instead, "making void the word of God by your own tradition" (*Mark 7:11-13*). Our Lord can do no less today, for not only the Faith, but natural reason teaches that the debt owed to parents can never be paid off, the gift of life being both priceless and eternal. And now the same children who forswear their elders will justify limiting the number of their own progeny under the pretext of making the world a better place for them!

Every social evil was loosed upon the world by Cain's city. Biblical prototype of all the utopias man would invent on his own without God's help, Cain's city was the consequence of that most antisocial of sins, the murder of a brother deemed "undesirable." Murder and utopia have maintained close relations ever since, and today, whether in the form of abortion, contraception, euthanasia, concentration camps or the sterilization or elimination of the unfit, murder is emerging ever more and more openly as a tool of choice in forging the utopian society of the future. According to Hebrew tradition Cain himself was murdered by his descendant, the cruel and bloodthirsty Lamech, who mistook him for a wild beast while hunting.

Already Lamech had, introduced polygamy into society, and by his unlawful second wife Sella (a name meaning "shadow"), had fathered the bastard Tubalcain, "who was a hammerer and artificer in every work of brass and iron" (*Gen. 4:22*). Their unhallowed union thus proved the fountainhead of the science and technology which materialism inevitably produces, and on which it must feed to survive. We are told that eventually men became so wicked that "all the thought of their heart was bent upon evil at all times" (*Gen. 6:5*), until finally everything was swept away by the merciful waters of the Flood.

Generations later, after Noah's sons had repopulated a purified earth which was still "of one tongue, and of the same speech", the men of Babel resurrected Cain's experiment. By this time their science and technology was considerably advanced, for Scripture tells us its builders "had brick instead of stones, and slime instead of mortar," the natural construction materials created by God having been replaced by artificial ones produced by their own ingenuity. With these in hand the sons and heirs of Cain were determined to "make their name famous," not only by building a city, but especially by raising the famous Tower whose top would reach heaven.

We know what happened. Taking cognizance of their intent, God says, "They have begun to do this, neither will they leave off from their designs, till they accomplish them in deed," so, exercising His mercy once more, He disrupted all communication by confusing their tongues. "They ceased to build the city," and scattered over the face of the earth, taking the old utopian dream with them wherever they went (*Gen. 10:1-8*).

+

Such was the plight of mankind until the Son of God arrived to lay the groundwork of His eternal Kingdom on our vitiated earth. As soon as men heard about it, some were so enthusiastic that they planned to force Him to be their king, and He had to hide from them (*John 6:15*). After His Ascension into heaven, however, where He sits at the right hand of the Father, He sent the Holy Ghost, through whose power the faith spread like wind-driven fire throughout the

Roman Empire. That political giant was before long baptized and re-assembled into the Holy Roman Empire, and for centuries men were led to hope that someday they might all be one here below after all. The most diverse peoples communicated with one another within it, sharing not only the true religion, but two common languages and a flexible code of law. Myriad cultures grew and thrived. Civilization overflowed the Empire's borders and beyond, as tribe after distant tribe became Christianized and prospered in the climate of the Faith.

One reason the Empire endured as long as it did is that it was an empire. It provided the viable structure for common life at all levels which only an empire can provide. The history of the world has many times demonstrated that mere nationalism is never enough, at least not for long. It seems that nations are not naturally constituted to stand alone any more than Adam; they preserve their vitality best where they are associated with other nations in that easy marriage of unity and freedom based on hierarchy which an empire best allows. The only exception to this rule was the little Hebrew nation, which succeeded in standing alone, but only because it enjoyed the special help of God in view of its special role in the economy of salvation.

As a matter of fact, the Holy Roman Empire functioned so well for so long, its citizens tended to think of it as coeval with the Church. Certainly it was informed by her divine doctrine, but it was not of divine institution. The greatest lesson to be learned from the Holy Roman Empire is that it failed. Like any other human institution, it was mortal and could not subsist beyond its appointed time in the face of the sins of men. Theoretically feasible, a permanent Christian economy of that kind in this world is morally impossible. It is impossible for the same reason that the just man sins seven times a day despite his best efforts, for the same reason that St. Paul gave when he acknowledged, "The good which I will, I do not; but the evil which I will not, that I do" (*Rom. 7:15*).

Progressively shattered by schism, heresy, revived paganism and triumphal atheism, political Christendom is no more. Today we watch in consternation as the beneficent flood waters of Christian culture it let loose over the world slowly recede, leaving men's souls everywhere dry and desolate. Out of sheer desperation the members of Christ's Mystical Body have allowed themselves to be drawn into the only substitutes for Christendom they can find today:

first the League of Nations, then the United Nations, with far more sophisticated forms of manmade unity being proposed for the immediate future.

Only God can create a perfect society. He did so when His only-begotten Son set the Holy Catholic Church on earth in our midst. It is eternal, yet in the hearts of men; in the world, but not of it. Like everything God has created, whether angelic or material, natural or supernatural, the Church is hierarchical, not egalitarian. To make the world safe for democracy is literally to declare war upon her. When our Lord told Pilate the politician, "My kingdom is not of this world," He informed him at the same time that he would have no authority whatever unless it had been given to him from above.

The gates of hell will never prevail against the Church as they did against Christendom. It is a Nation above all other nations, their supreme Mother and Teacher here below. Sufficient unto itself, without spot or wrinkle, its citizens are divinely chosen, predestined, governed and set apart by God in a far higher sense than the little Jewish nation which prefigured it. It is an article of our Creed that we believe in this Holy Catholic Church and in all her divine attributes: one, holy, universal and apostolic. These marks are neither invisible nor merely spiritual. They are embedded in the here and now, where they can be seen and touched and heard. Hers alone is the supreme government of the world.

There are those who speak of rebuilding the Holy Roman Empire which was Christendom, as if this were in their power. Like the Jews they too long for a temporal Messianic kingdom of this world, albeit in Christian dress. As the situation of the world grows worse, this hope does not die, but only gathers momentum. At bottom it is nothing but utopianism in a particularly dangerous form, for in view of its heavy disguise, it easily passes itself off as Catholic. There is no political solution to mankind's problems, not now any more than in our Lord's day. As Pius XI pointed out in *Quadragesimo Anno*, there can be no social reconstruction of any kind which is not preceded by Christian renewal in the hearts of men.

In his aforementioned Motu Proprio, Benedict XV pinpoints the family, not the conference table, as the place to begin this reconstruction of society:

> *As the family constitutes the foundation of the human race,*
> *by strengthening domestic society with the bonds of purity,*
> *fidelity and concord, a new vigor and, as it were, new blood*
> *shall be diffused through all the members of human society*
> *under the vivifying influence of the virtue of Christ, nor shall*
> *the result consist merely in the correction of private morals, but*
> *even in the restoration of public and civil institutions.*

Still, the human weakness for utopia will undermine even the certainty of heaven. Because it has its roots in nostalgia for Eden, feeding daily on the wispy vestiges of Eden which still linger around us, our temptation to "the future now" will not go away. Knowing this, the devil need only continue to promise "all the kingdoms of the world" to persuade men to bow down and worship him (*Matt. 4:8-9*). Whoever succumbs serves him willy-nilly. Even the best men yearn to be happy here and now, because men were made for happiness. At the Transfiguration on Mount Thabor, St. Peter, all the while hearing Moses and Elias speaking with our Lord about His approaching Passion, couldn't help exclaiming, "It is good for us to be here; let us make three tabernacles !" Here, now! To which Scripture adds, "not knowing what he said" (*Luke 9:31-33*).

THE SIN OF UTOPIA

At Fatima the Mother of God divulged some very serious information regarding Russia. She didn't call this nation the Union of Soviet Socialist Republics, the name by which it came to be commonly known. In this name would be spread the deadly errors which she was warning her children were already being spread "in every country, raising up wars and persecutions against the Church," making martyrs and annihilating whole nations. Ah, we are told, but of course our Lady wouldn't refer to the USSR back in 1917, when most people wouldn't even know what she was talking about.

Not so. This cannot be the reason. The powers to whom her message was primarily addressed knew very well what she was talking about. Furthermore, in the course of the apparitions she mentioned the name of Pius XI, a future Pope not yet elected and unknown to all. It is far more likely that she called the nation Russia because that is its true identity under God, whereas the Soviet Union is only a concoction of men, in which God had no share. As a political concept, this so-called Union stands outside reality. It is a phantasm, or if you will, a nightmare. Even at this writing it is undergoing change.

By now the world has grown used to artificial nations. When several were suddenly catapulted into the news by the war in the Persian Gulf, they occasioned no surprise. Since the Treaty of Versailles it is generally believed that nations are the fruit of human deliberation. In the name of "self-determination of peoples," whole litters of cross-bred, man-made, independent countries began proliferating after World War I and continue until now.

Some, like Kuwait and its neighbors which were pried loose from the defeated Ottoman Empire, had very ancient pedigrees and had boasted great cities. One was Nineveh in modern Iraq. Not only did Jonas the prophet preach repentance to it, but the Son of God warned, "The men of Nineveh shall rise in the judgment with this generation, and shall condemn it" (*Matt. 12:41; Luke 11:32*). The fulfillment is not yet, but Nineveh waits patiently, its remains subsisting today near the little town of Mosul. Let "this generation" which is always with us beware, for Christ's words do not pass away.

Not that tradition was a prime consideration in the manufacture of nations, for some were manufactured out of whole cloth. From the remains of Austria-Hungary, the other great empire to fall to the forces of democracy in 1918, were produced *in vitro* monsters like Czechoslovakia and Yugoslavia. And there were Lebanon and Vietnam. After World War II, with the progressive dismemberment of the remaining European colonial empires, still others were set up in Asia and Africa, with no end in sight.

All have been successively hailed as harbingers of the world utopia envisioned first under the League of Nations and now under the United Nations. After more or less agonized bursts of freedom, some of the newly hatched nations with the made-to-order names found themselves incorporated into the aforesaid Union of Soviet Socialist Republics, but no matter, for these are only formative stages. In Helsinki at the beginning of the decade of the 90's, the President of the United States opined, "If the nations of the world, acting together, continue as they have been, we will set in place the cornerstone of an international order more peaceful than any we have known."

+

And who should know better than the American President? Doesn't the whole world confess the inspired wisdom of those English revolutionaries who put together the United States of America, acknowledged pioneer among artificial governments? The Americans also pioneered the nuclear bomb and were the first to drop it. Their immediate target happened to be Japan, a nation on the other side of the Pacific which still languished under the rule of an Emperor venerated as divine. Surrendering unconditionally to so unprecedented a chastisement, the Japanese were not long in adopting more democratic ways, and soon basked in the material benefits which followed on their enlightenment.

In many ways the new bomb was the material counterpart of the first one the Americans exploded over Christendom in 1776. When they decided to govern themselves in their own name, without reference to authority monarchical or ecclesiastic, at a time when nearly everyone believed God to be the evident source of all authority, they let loose shock waves which have not subsided to this day. The old political landscape has been so leveled and the landmarks left standing so few, it is hard to identify the damage, let alone assess it.

Their Declaration of Independence was formal:

We hold these truths to be self-evident: That all men are created equal; that they are endowed by their Creator with certain unalienable rights; that among these are life, liberty and the pursuit of happiness. That, to secure these rights, governments are instituted among men, deriving their just powers from the consent of the governed; that, whenever any form of government becomes destructive of these ends, it is the right of the people to alter or to abolish it, and to institute a new government, laying its foundations on such principles, and organizing its powers in such form, as to them shall seem most likely to effect their safety and happiness.

From these words the revolutionary mentality leaps fully armed, like Athena from the brain of Zeus. To be sure, the gentlemen who promoted this scandalous document didn't get such ideas out of thin air, and certainly not from the French Grand-Orient. It was rather the other way round, for they had germinated in Judaism via Protestantism and had festered in their mother country ever since the days of Cromwell, who unofficially permitted the Jews to return to England, whence they were proscribed in 1290. Bossuet, the great Bishop of Meaux and defender of the Faith under Louis XIV, says Cromwell overturned the monarchy simply by mobilizing a "limitless mixture of sects."

The American English would be the first to succeed in translating the aspirations for religious freedom into political terms. Not only would men enjoy freedom of conscience where religion was concerned, but they would be free to govern themselves in any way "as to them seemed most likely," because according to them, political authority is derived exclusively "from the consent of the governed." If the governed become dissatisfied with their regime, well, according to their Declaration, "it is the right of the people to alter or abolish it."

As de Tocqueville sagely noted, "With democratic nations, each new generation is a whole new people." The United States in particular has become known as a nation without memory. Like the weather in Washington, D.C., if you don't like it, just wait a minute. Armed with their Declaration, the American fathers first provided themselves with an arrangement known as the Articles of Confederation. As these were found wanting almost immediately, they were forthwith "altered and abolished" and replaced by a more acceptable Constitution. Not surprisingly, the opening words of this document are "We the people."

Whereas the Declaration acknowledged an unspecified Creator as source of man's rights, nowhere is He mentioned in the Constitution. Why should He be, if government is entirely a human affair? The Constitution, as Judge Robert Bork pointed out, is merely a procedural document. As its preamble states, it is "ordained and established" by the people to "form a more perfect union, establish justice, insure tranquility, provide for the common defense, promote the general welfare and secure the blessings of liberty for ourselves and our posterity." The supernatural need have no place in such a program.

+

Voicing the general astonishment felt at the time, Joseph de Maistre marveled at man's new-found audacity. In *The Generative Power of Political Constitutions*, he says

> *He who has not the power even of making an insect or a blade of grass, believes that he is the immediate author of sovereignty, the most important, sacred and fundamental thing in the moral and political world ... He believed that he could constitute nations ... that he could create that national unity by virtue of which one nation is distinguishable from another.*

Incredible!
A nation is not a rational construction.

> *It is a truth as certain in its way as a mathematical proposition that no great institution results from deliberation, and that human works are fragile in proportion to the number of men concerned in them and the degree to which science and reasoning have been used* a priori.

Dictatorships or even hereditary monarchies set up by men cannot generate nations. He is in grave error who thinks that "such and such a family reigns because such and such a people has willed it; while he is surrounded by incontrovertible proofs that every sovereign family reigns because it is chosen by a superior power."

Nor does nationality consist in the common bloodlines we call race, for great nations have been composed of many races, some of them found at the same time in other nations. Often enough there is no common language. Not even a common religion can produce nationality. Nor is it the result of geographical location, nor a common history, nor even a common enemy, although all these elements contribute heavily. Above all, nationality is not the result of a common consent to live together under a written constitution. A government is not a nation. It may confer citizenship, but it is powerless to impart national character. Sometimes it becomes necessary to make a clear distinction between one's real country and one's legal country, when these have parted company, as Charles Maurras recommended in regard to the French republic.

St. Pius X tells us in *Vehementer*, "The Creator of mankind is also the Founder of human societies, and He preserves them just as He maintains individuals in existence." Underlying all man-made conglomerates are the "tribes and peoples and tongues and nations" seen in vision by St. John on Patmos and which only God can create (*Apo. 11:9*). "Only God can make a tree," and by the same token is a nation His handiwork, a living organism, capable of growth and activity, decline and decay. God sent Joan of Arc to make this clear. Her mission was precisely to establish the fact that France was a nation constituted by God under a king who was Jesus Christ's designated lieutenant. Neither the king of England, the Duke of Burgundy nor anyone else had any right, by treaty, hereditary claims or otherwise, to rearrange her politics or her boundaries. Not even France possessed such a right over herself.

Nations have vocations. Cardinal Pacelli, later Pius XII, declared at Notre Dame de Paris in July 1937, on the eve of World War II, "Like individuals, peoples are prosperous or unfortunate, influential or obscurely sterile to the degree that they are docile or rebellious to their vocations." He is said to have defined the nation as "that greater family given to us by God," saying that there was no surer sign of moral disorder than a decline in love for the national fatherland.

The artificial nation is a Frankenstein's monster which must sooner or later disintegrate into its component parts for want of the unifying principle only God can supply. We are witnessing this phenomenon on a grand scale in the world today. Man is not here to concoct governments and invent laws for himself. In politics as in everything else, his freedom is not absolute, but only a freedom of choice. "Our limits are the guardians of our strength and our unity," said Gustave Thibon. "We live within our limits as does blood within the artery, and opening the artery is no emancipation for the blood; a certain kind of political and scientific emancipation nevertheless resembles just that."

Man's pursuit of happiness here below consists in discovering the order which his Creator laid down for him and in conforming himself to it as closely as he can. Therein lies not only his temporal well-being, but his eternal destiny. Pius XII did not hesitate to say that on the conformation given to society hung both the welfare and the ruin of souls. We shall examine next what this conformation should be.

+

Until the eighteenth century theology was the obligatory crown of a proper education. Far from being an abstruse science reserved to churchmen and *periti*, theology was the common man's guidebook to reality. Until the Second Vatican Council, authoritative catechisms suited to every age and capacity put it within the grasp of all, to keep them from going astray in any area of life. Resting human reason on divine revelation, theology tells it like it is, not the way we think it should be. It is the one science of whose findings we can be certain.

Theology does not share the weakness of our modern scientific disciplines, which pile up mountains of slithering evidence but can prove nothing beyond the probable, because they are forced to proceed inductively. The conclusions of theology are hard, logical deductions derived from incontrovertible premises whose guarantor is almighty God. What contradicts it is pure illusion. By telling us what we are, how we got here, and where we are going, it tells us, among many other things, how we should be governed. This is all important, in view of where we may be heading.

Even Karl Mannheim saw the problem when he described utopianism as "an historical orientation transcending reality ... which, when it passes into conduct ... shatters the prevailing order." This is inevitable, for utopia is an intellectual fabrication with no organic relation to the real. It is a state of mind. Its declarations and manifestos do not even address themselves to any real persons, but only to "man" or to "humanity." In *Considerations on France* de Maistre writes:

> *There is no such thing as man in the world ... During my life, I have seen Frenchmen, Italians, Russians and so on; thanks to Montesquieu, I even know that one can be Persian; but I must say, as for man, I have never come across him anywhere; if he exists, he is completely unknown to me.*

Yet, for this non-existent creature a whole new world order is being set up under the new "religion of humanity.

In the final analysis, bad politics are the product of bad theology, the worst politics being the result of no theology. This is what revolution saddled us with when it separated the state from the Church, said Pius XII, and built its institutions on "nature without grace, on reason without faith, on liberty without authority and sometimes on authority without liberty ... First it cries, 'Christ yes, the Church no,' then 'God yes, Christ no,' then 'God is dead or maybe never existed.'"

St. John tells us in his Gospel that when the woman taken in adultery was brought before our Lord for judgment, He stooped down and wrote with His finger on the ground before He would make any comment. The Vulgate has, "*inclinans se deorsum digito scribebat in terra.*" He leaned down to write on the earth with His finger. In this apparently irrelevant action lies a parable of transcending import. Our Lord thereby showed the woman and her accusers how God from the heights of heaven writes the natural law into His material creation here below with the "finger of His right hand," the Holy Ghost.

There is an innate nature of things ordained by God when He made them, which determines not only their purpose, but reality itself. To flout nature or act contrary to it leads to delusion, madness, and eventually annihilation. In the case of the woman, it is clear that her adultery was sinful because it was an infraction of natural law. Nations in their political behavior may also break the natural law, with consequences far more ramified.

+

The law's ultimate source is the Most Blessed Trinity, exemplar, substratum and first cause of everything which exists, whether angelic, human or material. The closer anything conforms to the divine exemplar the greater its excellence, the more "real" it is. The less it conforms, the less its excellence, and the more it tends to nothingness. In the case of mankind, the Blessed Trinity is reproduced not only in the human individual made in Its image, but also in the human family, where father, mother and child represent naturally the divine Persons. This trinitarian group called the family is the basic cell of society, from which mankind increases and multiplies.

Only deranged minds would hold that all men, formed in the divine image, are created equal. The notion itself is silly. To be equal in the democratic sense one would at least have to be completely independent, and that is hardly the condition of contingent beings who share a common human nature and must eat to live. In faltering human language the divine Persons are described as co-equal and co-eternal, but theirs is no democracy. In the Godhead they subsist in a hierarchy of order, wherein the Father is ever the source of the other two, and in the family likewise, the father is always the head and source of life and authority.

Wrote Fr. J .M. Bauthier in *Le Sacrifice dans le Dogme Catholique*:

> *We dream of equal conditions as a panacea. That is folly. Besides the fact that such equality is desirable for no one, because it would lead to universal misery, it is furthermore radically impossible because it is contrary to nature. Nothing is on the same level in the works of God, and order has never consisted in the equality of beings, but in their harmony.*

At the root of inequality is God's wisdom: Although all men sprang from Adam and the earth, "With much knowledge the Lord hath divided them and diversified their ways" (*Ecclus. 33:11*).

Inequality is the very condition of their fruitfulness and indeed their happiness.

Inherent in this inequality is subsidiarity. This means that within an established hierarchy every part has its ordinary function, which may not be fulfilled by another. There are no identity crises in God's economy where everyone is somebody, just by the fact that he exists. Everyone has his place. He is not just "equal." He is much more than that. Superiors may not arrogate to themselves tasks which belong to subordinates, any more than inferiors may usurp higher authority. God showed the patriarch Jacob how angels moved upwards and downwards on the great mystical ladder "standing upon the earth, and the top thereof touching heaven" whereon the Lord himself "leaned" even as He spoke (*Gen. 28:12-13*), just as the Son leaned when He wrote on the ground before the woman taken in adultery.

Everyone has his special function in the traffic between heaven and earth. Under the universal intercession of our Lady and St. Joseph the Church designates particular saints as patrons over a great variety of human endeavors and encourages recourse to them. Nowhere is the revolutionary character of Protestantism better revealed than in its proud disregard for the mediation of our Lady, the angels, saints, clergy and fellow Christians in our dealings with our Creator. Its congenital refusal to accept the help of others in reaching God through the Communion of Saints, is rooted in an endemic intolerance of inequality. By sheer force of logic those who persist in this folly eventually arrogate divinity to themselves. Transferred to politics, such a mentality makes short work of subsidiarity. Whether the government is a republic or a democracy matters little.

In America violent tensions between the rights of the subsidiary states and those of the central government developed almost immediately with the Articles of Confederation. The hotly contested adoption of the Constitution was the first ominous victory for centralization. By the middle of the next century, one of the bloodiest civil wars in history - allegedly fought over slavery, but rightly defined as the War between the States - eventually decided the issue once more in favor of the federal government. The trend being irreversible, the central authority has become so powerful that now the country is ruled to an alarming extent by executive order pure and simple. By definition this is despotism, the normal term of democracy.

Democracy's congenital inefficiency would be sufficient to insure such an outcome. Speaking of economic support to the tottering USSR, Rear-Admiral Michel Berger pointed out that Communism is not just "intrinsically evil," but intrinsically inefficient, and declared that the only way to improve socialism was to get rid of it. His suggestion readily applies to all man-made governments. Despite its lofty egalitarian ideals, in practice it must resort to centralization, if only to get anything done. In Russia this is called "democratic centralism," but always it is directed by a small powerful nucleus. With variations depending on the nature and scope of the departure from natural law, the slide from democracy into slavery of one kind or another is a foregone conclusion.

+

It is laughable to think of democracy and communism as enemies, when actually they are stages of the same egalitarian error. If all men are equal, all must vote, for it is believed that he who votes rules. Fallen human nature being what it is, however, it soon becomes clear that he who owns is the one who rules. If equality is to be maintained, therefore all must also own, and there must be no private property. Thus does universal franchise lead to universal ownership, and democracy becomes socialism. The "errors of Russia" are natural derivatives of the errors of the United States, where, as the saying goes, "one man is as good as the next one, or a little better."

The fatal progression from democracy to slavery was foreseen by the Bishop of Meaux back in the days of Cromwell. In the funeral oration he delivered for King Charles' widow Queen Henrietta Maria he noted, "Once the means has been found to catch the crowd with the bait of liberty, they will follow blindly on merely hearing the word ... without seeing that they are heading for servitude." And again, "Where everyone may do as he pleases, no one does as he pleases; where there is no master, everybody is the master; where everyone is the master, everyone is a slave."

Cataloguing the evils unleashed by democracy would be tedious. One deserves special mention, however, for it reinforces all the others: It is compulsory education, a tyranny predicated on the delusion that if a man is literate he will know how to vote. This flies in the face of the fact that politics is a practical art, and that some of the world's greatest rulers have not known how to read or write. It is, however, a natural error for democracy to make, for democracy exists really only on paper. Apart from that, however, if all men are equal, they must be educated equally.

And here again, where everyone must be educated, no one is educated, because if the illusion of equality is to be maintained, the level of education must drop constantly to the lowest common denominator of taste and intelligence in order to accommodate everyone. Those capable of education cannot find it in egalitarian schools, because education by definition is a conforming of the intelligence to a progressive unveiling of reality. Being systematically deprived of truth and contact with reality, they cannot be educated.

Certainly they can be submitted to a high degree of conditioning, in the footsteps of Pavlov's dog. Like animals, they can be trained in any number of disciplines, even highly intellectual disciplines, because they are "thinking animals"; but again like animals, they cannot be educated, because under a government operating apart from God on principle, they do not know true liberty, which only knowledge of the truth can give. The fiction of equality would be truth's first casualty.

Education must now be sought outside the system, for it disappeared from the schools when it parted company with the Faith and lost its grip on reality. As a result, Americans today are offered instruction to the outer limits of their intelligence in everything from philosophy to underwater basket-weaving, with degrees to match. Many become extremely useful citizens and a credit to their country, but they are not educated. No matter how thorough or proficient, no matter how brilliant its accomplishments, instruction is not education.

Our institutions of higher learning are little more than expensive vocational schools where elaborate tools are acquired with a view to earning a living, and where truth is what works. In the lower grades, where schooling is forced on the student, he develops a "teach me if you dare" attitude which tends to continue throughout life and puts the responsibility for learning on the instructor rather than on the student where it belongs. Both are at the mercy of fixed curricula and operate in a morass of outside activities. Teachers are rather administrators. In cooperation with athletic coaches, social workers and psychologists, they can be counted on to steer the difficult student into acceptable channels. Not only is he not taught religion in the public schools, but he can be forbidden by law to pray during school hours, lest by addressing God he violate the sacred dictum separating Church and state.

According to that delightful libertarian Albert Jay Nock:

> *This is a far cry from the medieval Catholic universities, where the association of educable persons with them, and the exposure to the spiritual influences they generated, pretty well made up all there was to education. Here or there would emerge some great man, like Peter Abelard, John of Scotland, Bernard of Clairvaux, and aspiring youngsters out of all peoples, nations and languages would lay down the shovel and the hoe, pack up some provisions, tramp off and find them, camp down with them and pick up what they had to give; then tramp off to the next man whom they had heard of as mounting pretty heavy guns, and then the next.*

Democracy could never settle for anything like that.

+

Certain forms of government are incompatible with natural law. The errors of liberal democracy have been condemned by several Popes, and Communism was declared "intrinsically evil" by Pius XL Barring such exceptions, the Church has wisely never tied the Faith to any particular form of government, for many are possible and legitimate. This does not mean, however, that all are equal in excellence. Nor does it mean that sometimes imperfect forms are not better suited to particular times and circumstances. This was certainly true, for instance, of the Venetian Republic, which played so noble a part in the victory of Lepanto. It was also true of the Swiss Confederations. Some forms, however, are intrinsically better than others, *per se*, and their superiority can only reside in their closer conformity to natural law.

Pius VI declared monarchy to be " the best of governments." In *The Political Philosophy of Bl. Cardinal Bellarmine*, Fr. John Rager wrote in 1926:

> *Theoretically and in the abstract, it is indeed the most perfect form of government, for it is employed by the Creator of the universe; it is in accord with the natural propensity in all creatures towards rule by one; it was the government of God's chosen people in the Old Law; and it is the predominant factor in the constitution of Christ's Church in the new dispensation.*

Theology shows monarchy to be the one most closely patterned on the Godhead, one in which the king acts as father of the national family. As in the family, ruler and subjects in a monarchy are admittedly far from equal, where not even the citizens are equal to one another. As in heaven and the family, all subsist in a divinely established hierarchy of persons whose peace lies in their harmony. As in the family, the king is bound by the same natural law as his subjects, and like them he too must obey the laws of the nation. As Fr. Rager points out, "Monarchy in the hands of God is indeed a perfect system of government; in the hands of imperfect man, however, it is exposed to many defects and abuses." The divine right of kings as promoted by Henry VIII was one of them. Absolute monarchy is absolute heresy, and eventually it undermined the whole institution.

Because our kings are gone, it is harder now to see the deep reciprocity which exists between the family and the nation, and how the wounds of the one bleed from the other. Gone is that intermeshing inequality on which the welfare of both depended. Artificial nations are now breeding artificial families. These are "planned" not only as to the number and character of the progeny, but now any arbitrary arrangement of individuals living together (even sodomites) may figure as a family unit before the law, rearing "designer children" hatched from sperm banks. Feeding on one another, "planned communities" and groups of all kinds are setting up housekeeping outside reality. The old economy of love, based on a wealth of natural ties, is swallowed up in rules and regulations.

But this is only part of the story, which does not take into consideration its supernatural aspects. Infringement of the natural law alone could never account for the plight the world finds itself in today. After God became Man, a higher dimension was added to politics. Those human governments which by virtue of baptism became Christian were raised to the supernatural order and became subject to higher laws. In this respect the France of King Clovis, constituted under the Christian dispensation, was incomparably superior to Constantine's Roman Empire.

For the new nations of Christendom, conformity to natural law was only the substratum of good government. Along with their subjects, they had to assume the obligations which incorporation into the Mystical Body of Christ automatically conferred on them. Legislation thereafter had to take into account the supernatural destiny of its citizens, and not just their temporal welfare. The life of a nation would now be rooted in nothing less than the Communion of Saints.

If it is foolish to maintain that men are equal under natural law, it is madness to think they could be so in the supernatural order, where none is given grace equally, but only "according to the measure of the giving of Christ" (*Eph. 4:7*) and where Christians form part of one Body and possess only one Head. Although men and body parts are admittedly distinct, no one in his right mind would contend that all are equal, either in character or in function. St. Paul asks, "God has set the members every one of them in the body as it has pleased Him. And if they were all one member, where would be the body? Now you are the body of Christ, and members of member" (*1 Cor. 12:18-19, 27*).

In such a perspective, the ordinary pattern for society is not just the family, but the Holy Family, by means of which the divine exemplar, the Blessed Trinity, was literally brought to earth. In the family of Mary and Joseph, the Child is no mere representation of one of the Persons; He is actually and eternally the Son of God and the Second Person of the Godhead. In their household is found the very source, foundation and pattern of Christian politics. There is no other.

This being the case, the world's headlong descent into slavery can no longer be laid to the normal disruptions of original sin, for God has supplied a remedy. It must be laid to infidelity on the part of Christian nations to their supernatural obligations. Their whole *raison d'etre* is protecting the Holy Roman Catholic Church from her enemies and cooperating with her in the salvation of souls. Otherwise they have no reason to exist. Hear again Bossuet: "It is evident that inasmuch as separation and revolt from the Church was the source of all the evils, their remedies can be found only in a return to the unity and submission of yore."

The most perfect political society is the Monarchy called the Holy Roman Catholic Church. Not only is it directly derived from the Holy Family, to which it conforms both naturally and supernaturally (if not always in its members), but its Head is that Family's divine Son, to whom all power in heaven and on earth has been given by the Father. Born on Calvary from His riven side, the Church visibly reflects the hierarchy of the family and of the Godhead in her threefold configuration of priesthood, religious and laity, who act as one under the Son's earthly Vicar the Pope of Rome. As with the Persons of the Blessed Trinity these parts are distinct, but share a common nature within a hierarchy of order.

Yet the wonder is that - without detriment to her own organization or any subtraction from nations, races and classes - the Church always remains essentially a society of individual, mutually inhering persons. Given that persons are by definition incommunicable, this constitutes an unfathomable mystery. What is not possible to fallen humanity becomes possible in the Church, where God is the common bond through whom persons can communicate freely with one another here and in heaven.

Only in the Church is found that perfect equality which democracy proclaims, but of which it can produce only a sterile, diabolical image. This is why Marcel de Corte can call modern democracy, which differs radically from all classical and medieval democracies, a caricature of the Church. He goes so far as to declare it a specifically Christian heresy, one which could have arisen only among men who were acquainted with the perfect equality of persons first made possible by Christianity. As we have noted, in view of the new supernatural society, headed and animated by the Church, nations are mandated to provide temporal conditions which will promote not only their citizens' welfare on earth, but more important, their eternal happiness in heaven. The Church, Mother and Teacher of all nations, teaches them to pray that the will of their Father be done here on earth as it is in heaven. How is this possible if their governments do not first faithfully reproduce here on earth the divine pattern set for them by the heavenly hierarchies?

In *Summi Pontificatus*, Pius XII warned that governments "must not be founded on shifting standards of right and wrong, treacherous as quicksand, which have been arbitrarily devised to suit public and private interest. It must stand on the immovable rock of natural law and divine revelation." Such was the declared objective of King Clovis, whose Frankish kingdom, eldest daughter of the Church, was the cornerstone of that political miracle called Christendom. Setting the example, he consecrated France to Christ's Kingship forever by constitutional law. The document's preamble begins with, "The illustrious Nation of the Franks, having God for Founder," and closes by praying that, "the Lord Jesus Christ direct those who govern in the way of piety."

Apparently this was ratified in heaven, for generations later, at the height of France's apostasy, St. Pius X prophesied that "she who had made an alliance with God," would one day repent and "bear My Name before all peoples and all the kings of the earth." God's gifts being without repentance, we may believe that the return to natural law will begin with the conversion of regicide France.

+

Pope Pius VI had pointed out that Louis XVI had been guilty of no malfeasance, but had been executed for one reason alone: "because he was a king." Revolutionary antipathy for monarchy is consistent, and hardly accidental. The American Declaration of Independence is not merely a position paper. The larger part of the text is in fact a diatribe leveled against the" tyrant" George III, a good king who was not only indulgent to his subjects, but as it happens, violently opposed to the naturalistic aims of Freemasonry and well aware of the utopian forces at work in England as well as in its colonies.

Preoccupation with freedom from kings was a mask for the desire to be free of God. Enucleating its satanic core, Joseph de Maistre begins with a quotation from Job:

> *'Depart from us, God!' (21:14). Must we forever tremble before priests, and receive from them whatever instruction they care to give us? Throughout Europe, truth is hidden by the smoke of incense; it is time that it emerged from this fatal cloud. We shall no longer speak of you to our children; it is for them, when they become men, to decide whether You are and what You are and what You ask of them.*

All things displease us, because Your Name is written on all things. We wish to destroy everything and re-create it without Your help. Depart from our councils of state, our schools, our homes; we shall be better off alone, reason will be a sufficient guide. Depart from us, God!"

In due time, "every government and institution in Europe" would displease them:

...precisely because they were Christian; and in proportion to the influence of Christianity, a malaise of opinion, a general discontent seized men's minds. How has God punished this abominable delirium? He has punished it as He created the world, by a single phrase. He has said: LET IT BE - and the political world collapsed.

De Maistre penned these lines in the early 1800's. Today we see their truth only too clearly. Not only did collapse occur then, but it seems to continue interminably. Not an hour passes but something more flies loose, even to the hinges of the Church, now totally bereft of political protection. Do-it-yourself government brings in its wake a punishment which exquisitely fits the crime, for citizens who are free and equal cannot be expected to serve one another. Having abandoned the great trinitarian pattern of government on which unity and mutual cooperation depend, they are left to the mercy of a granulated economy, where the average man must look to machines for help.

Without time, training or talent for all the tasks of life, he is forced not only to govern himself (ironically enough, voting by machine), but as often as not to make his own house repairs with the aid of whatever hardware and manuals he can find. His leisure progressively disappears, and with it the cultural refinements that depend on it. Stress becomes unbearable. Unless he is rescued from on high, he can only sink deeper into misery, barbarism and frustration. As Origen said in *Contra Celsum*, "Nothing can be changed for the better in social matters without divine help." Left to his own fallen nature, man is incapable of reforming any human institution, because he cannot reform himself.

Yet, at the summit of his delirium, he insists that men are evil because their institutions are at fault, and he will cure society of its ills by creating new and perfect nations! Shortly after the outbreak of World War II, Pius XII wrote:

> *They boasted of progress, when they were in fact relapsing into decadence; they conceived that they were reaching heights of achievement when they were miserably forfeiting their human dignity; they claimed that this century of ours was bringing maturity and completion with it, when they were being reduced to a pitiable form of slavery. They had not the wit to see that any human effort to substitute for Christ's law or some base model of it, must prove altogether unfruitful.*

As the war raged on, in a radio message delivered on Christmas Eve in 1944, this same Pope had this to say about artificial nations:

> *The state does not contain in itself and does not mechanically gather within a given territory an amorphous agglomeration of individuals. The state is, and must be in reality, the organic and organizing unity of a true people ... Equality degenerates into a mechanical leveling, into a drab uniformity: the sentiment of true honor, personal commitment, respect for tradition, dignity - in a word, all that gives life its true value - little by little sinks and disappears.*

Yet the same men who think they can create nations also think they can make peace! Men who, according to Pius XII in *Summi Pontificatus*, "can only impose terms of peace on others" by force and terror. Alas, "There is no peace to the wicked" (*Is. 48:22*). De Maistre predicted: "There will be still more upheavals, and good order will not be thoroughly consolidated until either slavery or the true religion is restored." It cannot be otherwise for, "The great bulk of humanity is naturally in bondage, and cannot be rescued from this state except by supernatural means."

Nations are not useful conveniences. They are specifically mentioned thirteen times in the Apocalypse, along with a thrice-repeated promise that they shall be broken and "ruled with a rod of iron" by God's victorious Word (*2:27; 19:15; 12:5*). It is an ordinance of His providence that men are to be governed by other men, and this being the case, the probable character of His instruments is by now painfully clear. Only His Mother's promise that her Immaculate Heart will triumph in the end makes the prospect bearable. Our political situation is now so desperate the only supernatural means open to us is the merciful intercession which she offered us at Fatima. The freedom to accept it is one of the few freedoms we have left. If it is rejected, the gulag need only widen its jaws to accommodate the whole of Utopia's bedazzled inhabitants.

ST. JOAN CONFRONTS UTOPIA

Only divine intervention can arrest the craze for utopia, rooted as it is in the divine image in which we were created. Because it is part of our human nature to crave unity- and want things just right, putting society straight is a standing temptation. Watching the men at work on the tower of Babel, God prophesied they would never "leave off from their designs till they accomplish them in deed" (*Gen. 11:3-6*). Nor have they. In our own day, James P. Warburg, scion of the international banking family, told a Senate committee meeting in 1950, "We shall have world government whether you like it or not - if not by consent, by conquest!"

Unfortunately, when fallen human nature seeks political unity on its own, without reference to divine law, it goes nowhere, as should be suspected from the very meaning of the word utopia. God doesn't confront this kind of madness by reasoning, because unbridled reason is precisely what causes it in the first place. The lunatics of Babel, trying to reach heaven through technology and "make their name famous," were not to be stopped by argument, but only by a catastrophic disruption of their communications systems, which struck without warning or recourse.

It is therefore not surprising that centuries later, when the ambition of the English kings threatened Christendom with a new world order of their own making, God acted again in similar fashion. Without preamble He confronted the erring utopians with Joan of Arc, a sturdy peasant girl of seventeen, hardly five feet tall. In 1429 she appeared suddenly before Charles, the beleaguered heir to the French throne, wearing men's clothing, her black hair cut short, and there was no getting around her. She told him she had orders from God to see him properly crowned and to stop the English in their tracks.

There is nothing legendary about Joan. Although no contemporary portrait of her exists she is probably the best documented saint of all time. Rather than dig for information, her biographers must plow out from under it. Volumes of testimony from her own lips and from witnesses who knew her were collected at her trial in Rouen, and still more was produced at the judicial proceedings which exonerated her a generation after her death. We know who her family were even to her godparents, what she wore, what she ate, who her childhood friends were. Every detail of her public life, her miracles, her tears, her prowess with the lance and her love of fine armor and horseflesh are all on record.

There is no human explanation for Joan's victory over the English. It began when Charles' advisors finally allowed her to write them a letter. Admitting that she couldn't "tell A from B," she dictated it to the royal notaries. Dated Tuesday in Holy Week 1429, the letter is superscribed with the names Jhésus-Maria, and addressed bluntly to "the King of England, and you the Duke of Bedford, who call yourself regent of the kingdom of France; you, William de la Pole, Earl of Suffolk; you, John Lord Talbot; and you, Thomas Lord Scales, who call yourselves lieutenants of the aforementioned Duke of Bedford."

She summons these lords to no conference table, but to "give satisfaction to the King of Heaven." She commands them to "deliver the keys of all the goodly towns you have taken and violated in France to" no less a person than herself, whom she designates as:

> *...the virgin who has been sent by God the King of Heaven ... Go back, for God's sake, to your own country; otherwise expect to hear from the virgin who will soon visit you to your great detriment. King of England, if you don't do this, I am the commander-in-chief, and wherever I find your people in France, I'll force them to leave willy-nilly, and if they won't obey, I'll have them all killed. I am sent here by God ... to boot you out of France! King Charles, the true heir, shall have her, for God the King of Heaven wills it.*

Obviously, Joan was no peacenik. She closes by begging the Duke of Bedford not to force her to destroy him, but rather to join forces with her in "the greatest feat ever accomplished for Christendom." Unfortunately, the English didn't take her seriously. They should have known better, for their own soothsayer Merlin and one of their saints, the Venerable Bede, contributed two of the many prophecies in circulation at the time which foretold that a virgin warrior would miraculously heal the wounds of Europe.

She herself testified, "Hasn't it been foretold that France, lost through a woman, would be saved by a woman?" The woman who ruined France was Isabelle, daughter of the French king Philippe le Bel and wife of Edward II of England. By claiming the French throne for her son Edward III in defiance of salic French law - which recognized no succession through the female line - Isabelle started a dispute between the two countries which developed into the Hundred Years War.

The French recognized this war as a divine chastisement, brought on by the sins of Philip, who had gone so far as to drag Boniface VIII from the papal throne in his attempt to subject the Church to his political ambitions. After 75 years of humiliating defeats and foreign occupation, the French were reduced to public prayer, penance and processions. Finally, in 1412 Joan was born in the little village of Domremy in the marches of Lorraine. The day was Epiphany, feast of the Three Kings, the world's first monarchs to acknowledge Christ's royal supremacy. Extraordinary signs accompanied her birth, and she began enjoying mystical experiences at a very early age.

When she was thirteen Saint Michael the Archangel informed her that she had been chosen by the King of Heaven to save the kingdom of France. He also told her that she must wear masculine clothing, because "You shall bear arms and become the head of the army; all things shall be guided by your counsel." Alarmed by such a communication, the girl told no one, but it was only the beginning of a long series of visions which continued to the day of her death five years later, when she was burned at the stake in Rouen.

St. Michael was joined by hundreds of angels, but principally by St. Catherine and the primitive St. Margaret, who transmitted the orders from heaven. Asked at her trial why they didn't speak English, Joan retorted, "Why should they, when they were on the French side?" As to whether or not St. Michael appeared to her naked she replied, "Do you suppose our Lord didn't have the wherewithal to clothe him?" Sharp repartee and sound common sense of this kind characterized all Joan's utterances.

She had arrived at the eleventh hour, for France was perishing as a nation, bled white from prolonged warfare on her soil. Her worst problem was intestine for many of the French lords, following the lead of the regent, the powerful Duke of Burgundy, were openly collaborating with the enemy. With constant pillaging and looting on both sides, crops couldn't be sown or harvested, and famine threatened. Joan's own village, loyal to the king, was burned at least once by Anglo-Burgundian neighbors. Morality was at low ebb. As the king of England remarked to his French prisoner, the Duke of Orleans, "I hear that such sensuality, sin and evil vices have never been seen as now in France ... It's no wonder God is wroth."

Joan was eight years old when the worst happened: after the French rout at Agincourt the Treaty of Troyes was signed between Henry V of England and Charles' father, poor mad Charles VI. Juridically, France was terminated, for according to its terms, Henry V would marry Catherine, daughter of Charles VI, on whose death France and England would merge under the English crown. When Charles VI died two years later, England promptly entered into legal possession. Further resistance on the part of the French was hampered by the fact that the heir Charles VII was himself uncertain of the legitimacy of his succession. Presumably with his mother Queen Isabeau's acquiescence, the treaty had actually referred to him as the "so-called Dauphin," as if he were a bastard excluded from public affairs.

At this point, like a bolt from the blue, the little peasant girl's Voices told her it was time to acquaint Charles with heaven's plans. As Joan's admiring contemporary, the lyric poetess Christine de Pisan would put it, "In 1429 the sun began to shine!" Her meeting with Charles was, to say the least, extraordinary. Forewarned of her purpose, he was understandably wary. He disguised his royal person as one of his own courtiers, but Joan easily picked him out of the crowd and informed him, "Gentil Dauphin, my name is Jehanne la Pucelle," literally, "My name is Joan the virgin." The word *gentil* in that day did not mean" gentle" in the modern sense of "gentleman," but rather "national," or even "racial." Without more ado she told him, "The King of Heaven sends me to you with the message that you shall be anointed and crowned in the city of Reims, and that you shall be the lieutenant of the King of Heaven, who is the King of France."

Charles insisted she was mistaken and pointed out one of his lords as the king. "In God's name, noble prince," Joan exclaimed, "it is you and no other!" On the spot she assured him, "I tell you in the name of our Lord that you are the true heir of France and the son of the King!" In one sentence she disposed not only of his doubts regarding his legitimacy, but she made it clear that heaven upheld the salic law forbidding succession through a female line.

The Treaty of Troyes Joan dismissed as null and void, for the simple reason that the king of France had no authority whatever to dispose of his crown, which under the national constitution established by King Clovis belonged not to him, but to Christ. The bystanders reported that Charles, after speaking with her, looked as if he had been visited by the Holy Ghost. Privately she had reminded him of three requests he had made of God on All Saints Day, requests he had not discussed even with his confessor.

Thunderstruck at the revelation of his most secret thoughts, Charles was convinced of her authenticity. It has been surmised that he had asked, first, that if he were not the true heir, he should no longer be the cause of prolonging the war; second, that he alone, and not the people, should be punished if the present adversities were due to his sins; and third, that if the sins of the people were the cause, that they should be forgiven.

Despite her guarantee that St. Louis and Charlemagne were praying for him before the throne of God, Charles was not one to act rashly. His mother-in-law the Queen of Sicily was enjoined with her ladies to verify the sex and virginity of Joan, who was furthermore subjected to lengthy questioning by learned doctors and divines of the University of Poitiers. One of the inquisitors tried to trip Joan by remarking, "You say your voices tell you that God wishes to free the people of France from their present calamities. But if He wishes to free them, it's not necessary to have an army." To which Joan, out of patience, retorted, "In God's name, the soldiers will fight, and God will provide the victory!"

The military campaign which ensued has no counterpart in history. Leading the king's troops to Orleans, under siege for over six months by the Duke of Bedford - who was financing his campaign with funds given to the Cardinal of Winchester by Pope Martin V to fight the Hussites - Joan struck like lightning. Her overall strategy, an unrelenting offensive allowing the enemy no time to rally, achieved its objective primarily by dissolving his morale. Between the time she was presented to the king on March 10, and when he was anointed at Reims on July 17, she reclaimed not only Orleans, but seven other towns, and captured the Earl of Suffolk and Lord Talbot as well.

Joan was known to remain in armor for six days running, a feat hardly equaled by the toughest knights. A master tactician, she excelled in the deployment of artillery. Seasoned veterans were astounded at the accuracy of her judgment in combat. Military experts have studied her methods without being able to unlock her secret, yet her secret is an open one: she acted only under orders from heaven. On one occasion, when her captains had decided among themselves to await reinforcements before launching a major at- tack, she declared, "Well, you've had your meeting, and I've had mine. And believe me, our Lord's advice will produce results, whereas yours will produce nothing!" And so it happened.

She possessed infused knowledge, discernment of spirits and the gift of prophecy to a high degree. She even raised a dead child to life. The very sword she carried was a mysterious one discovered by her revelation, buried behind the altar of the church of St. Catherine at Fierbois, believed to have been the one by which Charles Martel repelled the Mohammedans. After she broke it on the back of a camp follower she was driving away from the men, it could never be repaired, and disappeared from history. It is regrettable that her military exploits overshadow her long hours of prayer, her fasts, her charity to the poor and her abundant tears. She habitually prepared her men for battle by requiring them to go to Confession and receive Holy Communion. When she approached Orleans riding a favorite white charger, it was to the singing of the *Veni Creator*.

Before her went her banner, no mere national emblem or royal colors, much less a battle flag, but a standard hung at center from a pole, like those used in religious processions. It had been made to order by a Scotch painter at Tours named Hamish Power (in French, *Hauves Poulvoir*). On a white field spangled with golden fleurs-de-lys, alongside the names Jhésus-Maria, was enthroned the figure of Christ the King holding the world in His hand and flanked by two angels. At her trial she deposed, "I loved my sword, but I loved my standard forty times more. The whole thing was ordered by our Lord, by the voices of St. Catherine and St. Margaret, who told me 'Take up the standard for the King of heaven. Take it boldly, and God will help you.'"

Orleans was delivered within the octave of the Ascension, the feast which above all others commemorates the victory of Christ the King, for it is on that day He entered heaven to claim His eternal throne. A miraculous flooding of the river Loire which kept the English at bay, had allowed the French to enter the city and provision it, and on the vigil of the feast the first enemy fortification fell. Ascension Day was spent, not in battle, but in prayer, and by the next Saturday the last cordon was breached and the city liberated.

Because the following day was Sunday, Joan forbade her troops to fight unless they were attacked, but there was no danger of that. English resistance was broken. The enemy simply left, and Joan didn't pursue them. "Ah well, let them go," she said. "And we'll thank God, for today is Sunday." It was also the eighth day of May, feast of her commanding officer and heavenly counterpart, St. Michael the Archangel.

With the deliverance of Orleans a spell had been broken. Knights from all over the continent began rallying to Charles' cause, which everyone now seemed to recognize as God's own. The way cleared for his coronation as if by magic, for on July 16, feast of Our Lady of Mt. Carmel, the city of Reims, till then an ally of the English, submitted without a fight. At Joan's insistence the ladies of the town worked all night preparing the royal robes so the ceremony could take place the following day in the historic cathedral.

With Joan and her banner at his side, the Dauphin, wearing the dalmatic of a sub-deacon beneath the royal mantle, was duly anointed by the Archbishop of Reims, successor to St. Remi who anointed Clovis. The same miraculous chrism which had anointed Clovis was used, and which continued to be used for all the French kings down to the last one, Charles X. There were nine anointings in all, on head, hands, shoulders and elbows, as in the ritual for a bishop, for the King of France is no ordinary monarch. As Christ's vicar in the temporal order in the royal line of David, he partakes in an eminent way of the Kingship which Christ received from His eternal Father. His enemies would be pleased to forget that the very word Christ, *Christos*, means "anointed."

At the close of the ceremony, which lasted nine hours, the cathedral resounded with a blare of trumpets and shouts of *"Noël! Noël!"* and Charles was crowned. Neither Constantine nor Theodosius ever received such a consecration, conferred like Holy Orders during the Holy Sacrifice of the Mass. Years before, Charles had proclaimed himself king at his residual capital south of the Loire at Bourges, but only now did Joan address him as such. Falling at his feet, she clasped his knees and exclaimed with tears, "Gentil king, now is God's will done!" Many wept with her.

That very day she wrote a letter to the Duke of Burgundy begging him to be reconciled with his liege lord:

> *I beseech you, with my hands joined, on the part of the King of Heaven ... my true and sovereign Lord, that you cease warring with the Holy Kingdom of France ... All who war against this said Holy Kingdom of France are at war with the King Jesus, King of Heaven and the whole world!*

Alas, the rebellious Duke didn't give up that easily. Joan urged Charles to press immediately to the capture of Paris and the rest of northern France, but grown confident with success, he soon began listening to treacherous advisors who counseled him to turn to diplomacy rather than continue to rely on the sword. For Joan, military combat and diplomacy were not interchangeable or even complementary modes of warfare, as students of Clausewitz or Lenin would one day lead the world to believe. For her they were quite distinct from each other, with no blurred edges. The very concept of a "cold war" would have been incomprehensible to her.

She assured the king, "Peace cannot be had but at the point of a lance!" Unfortunately he wasted valuable time temporizing with the enemy. When he finally ordered the attack on Paris, it failed, and Joan was wounded. After that confidence in her began to wane, and her advice was disregarded. For the most part the campaign continued without her, although a month before her capture at Complegne, she was still begging the king, "Put me to work, for I won't last much longer, a year at the most!"

After less than a year in the field, her Voices had told her that it was God's will that she be captured. The most arduous part of her earthly mission would begin after her Burgundian captors sold her to the English. France's chastisement would be suspended and Christendom saved for a time, but only at the price of a year in prison spent in physical and moral agony, subject to unremitting interrogation and every indignity. Whatever remained to be done would be accomplished not by the sword, but by immolation to the divine will:

"I well know," she said, "that the English will kill me, thinking to win the kingdom of France after my death; but were there 100,000 more *Godons* than there are now, they shall not have the kingdom!" Here Joan used the popular French nickname for the English which was derived from their favorite expletive, *Goddam.* She predicted that within seven years Charles would regain Paris and that England "would end by losing France. I'm telling you this so that when it happens, you will remember I said so."

+

Joan was burned in the market place at Rauen on the vigil of Corpus Christi and canonized on the spot by her terrified executioner, who cried out, "We have burned a saint!" At the foot of the stake he had found her heart, entire and still beating, and despite liberal applications of oil and sulfur, he was unable to reduce it to ashes. In desperation he threw it with whatever else remained of her into the river and ran to the Dominican friary to find a priest to hear his confession. There were relics of Joan's heavenly visitors, St. Margaret's at Troyes and St. Catherine's at Rauen, but Joan would leave none.

It has now been proved fairly conclusively that she never made any retraction of any kind. This would appear to have been a fabrication of her enemies, never believed at the time. The alleged abjuration which was entered into the minutes was very, very long, whereas according to eyewitnesses the paper Joan signed was only six or seven lines, whereby she agreed not to wear men's clothes or her hair short, and not to carry weapons. Even this she qualified by "insofar as it was God's will." And it must be remembered that Joan was illiterate.

Her sanctity was so generally recognized, there is no record of any prayers or Masses ever having been offered for her. Spontaneously people began praying to her, and they have continued to do so ever since. From the beginning she was the object of universal veneration, with an obsessive fascination for the English. John Tressart, secretary to the King of England, declared, "We are lost!" Catholics like the French, the English had to discredit Joan as a false visionary, lest it be proved that God was against them. She was brought before no secular court to be accused of war crimes or political offenses, but before an ecclesiastical court for crimes against the Faith. Her conviction for heresy, in those days rightly considered a crime against the state, constituted. an indirect condemnation of the French monarchy as well.

In due time a papal decree would declare the trial illegal in every respect. Without going into details, suffice it to say that Bishop Cauchon had been chosen as her judge on the pretext that she had been captured in his diocese. (He was Bishop of Beauvais, and Joan was captured in his city of Compiegne.) A tool of the English, he had been the foremost architect of the Treaty of Troyes, an agreement which re-arranged the political structure of Europe to suit the conquerors and laid the foundations of the whole new world order they had in mind. The assessors were nearly all from the University of Paris, hotbed of utopianism. It was not so much Joan, as the English concept of utopia which was on trial. Her conviction meant its vindication.

The last part of her trial was conducted privately in her prison, for there was too much sympathy for Joan in open court. An English lord who was present was heard to exclaim, "If only she were English!" Unfortunately for them she was not, so she died wearing a paper headdress on which were inscribed the words: "Heretic, relapsed, apostate, idolatress." Wishing to destroy her good name, "perfidious Albion" glorified her with martyrdom and gave her to us all. The collect of her Mass reads, "God, who marvelously raised up the blessed virgin Joan to defend the Faith and the fatherland, grant through her intercession that Thy Church, victorious over the snares of the enemy, may enjoy peace without end."

Obviously the trouble Joan was sent to settle was no mere territorial squabble between two rival nations. At stake was the world's equilibrium. From the Three Kings on down, all civil rulers owe allegiance to Christ the King, but foremost among them is the king of France. According to Pope Gregory VII, "The kings of France are superior to other monarchs as are sovereigns to private citizens," - a pronouncement Gregory IX would confirm in a famous letter to St. Louis IX wherein he refers to France as the new tribe of Judah.

It reads:

As in ancient times the tribe of Judah received a special blessing from on high among the sons of the patriarch Jacob, so the kingdom of France is above all other peoples, crowned with extraordinary prerogatives by God himself. The tribe of Judah was the prefiguration of the kingdom of France. The Redeemer ... hangs it as a quiver about His loins from which He draws chosen arrows ... Thus, He chose France in preference to all other nations of the earth for the protection of the Catholic

*faith. For this reason France is God's own kingdom, and the
enemies of France are the enemies of Christ.*

Joan insisted that she had come "for the poor, for the little
people." By the simple expedient of restoring the rights of Christ
the King over France, she held back for five centuries the godless
utopia which is engulfing them today. Being illiterate, she left no
written doctrine. Her actions, however, are eloquent. She never
attacked her adversary without first manifesting the justice of her
cause and inviting him to give satisfaction. When this was refused,
she had no scruples about using force. Once he surrendered, she
didn't pursue him or exact reprisals. She sought no revenge beyond
obtaining her objective, and brought no charges against the defeated
for alleged "war crimes."
    In the end she forfeited her life rather than deny that God takes
sides in warfare even as He does in politics. Disputes between
nations, as between individuals, are not mere" conflicts of interest,"
but involve right and wrong. It is not legality which determines
what is right, but conformity to divine law, both natural and
supernatural. Joan reaffirmed these truths not by preaching, and still
less by palavering at a conference table but, as she said, "at the point
of a lance!" There is no other way when the enemy has become deaf
to moral suasion.
    Throughout Europe, already the faith was giving way to
economics as the principle of unity. Commercial centers,
increasingly dominated by independent financial interests, began
amassing capital through usury. The old colonialism, which had
looked upon peoples as objects of conversion, began regarding
them as consumers or means of production. Printing had just been
invented, and the heretical ideas about to break out in the Council of
Basle were spreading like wildfire throughout the universities, won
to the naturalism of William of Ockham. Reason and mathematics
were re-forging objective reality. The Great Schism was only
recently healed, and the Turks were besieging Constantinople.
    Democracy was on the move. A hundred years before Joan
arrived on the scene, the Hussites had already coined the slogan
"Liberty, Equality and Fraternity," and the Moravians were
practicing Communism. In France, a lawyer named Pierre Dubois
had presented to Philippe le Bel a plan for international arbitration
by a wholly secular, representative body from which the Pope

would be specifically excluded. Not long after her death Podiebrad, king of Bohemia, won the support of several princes for setting up an international assembly very similar to the present United Nations. Voting by nation, it would have been empowered to apply sanctions against aggressors and enforce peace by military means.

God was on the side of the French because the English, deeply infected with the democratic ideas of John Wyclif, mentor of John Huss, were in the forefront of this secular revolution. Even in Paris the prestigious Sorbonne supported the English dream. It was no accident that the treaty of Troyes had been signed by everyone but the Pope! By mercantile and marital alliances Henry V already controlled three great capitals - London, Paris and Jerusalem - and was planning to reorganize Christendom under the English crown. Had France been absorbed by England at that time she would have been party to the anglican schism already in the making. All the other Catholic nations would have followed her into revolution, as eventually happened after 1789.

As it was, even England benefited from the reprieve, but as God warned at Babel, "They will not leave off from their designs till they accomplish them in deed." The island kingdom remained in the vanguard of utopianism, which could almost be called "the English heresy." In England the evil genius of Francis Bacon would forge both modern Freemasonry and the Royal Society, one the political, the other the scientific arm of secular revolution. It is no accident that in England Masonry is an arm of the Crown, whereas in Catholic countries it is an instrument of subversion.

From Bacon on down to the Fabians of the twentieth century, English utopianism often went underground, but never did it lose its momentum. As we have seen, by the end of the 18th century the English had succeeded in actually founding in their American colonies the world's first man-made government without ecclesiastical ties, modeled on the utopian Bensalem of Bacon's *New Atlantis.* All subsequent ones have been inspired by it, not excepting the French republic launched by Voltaire and the Encyclopedists, who derived their ideas from England.

It is now also known that the French Grand Orient, which actually put the Revolution in motion, was financed by British banks, grown powerful after Cromwell allowed the Jews back into England. Following the teachings of their famous rabbi Hillel, who died shortly after our Lord's Crucifixion, the Jews had no scruples regarding the practice of usury, strictly forbidden to Christians. Sustained by usury, Christ's enemies flourished economically. Now, after two world wars and the permanent establishment of an international authority, we are seeing the beginnings of the great society only dreamed of by the enemies of Joan of Arc. Slowly but surely, the unity of Christendom guaranteed by the Church is being replaced by a universal brotherhood of men held together exclusively by the Golden Rule!

The irony is, that unless the world had first known the blessings and glories of medieval Christian society, the modern international utopia could never have even been imagined, let alone attempted. Medieval society was truly democratic, truly international. In the days of Charlemagne a goatherd like Ebbon could become Archbishop of Reims without occasioning any surprise. National constitutions bound the monarch as well as the people, because laws were based on the Gospels. Autonomous groups flourished at all levels. Universities were truly universal. All nationalities taught a universal culture in a common language allowing boundless exchange of thought in all quarters.

As the great Lacordaire put it, freedom is old, it's despotism that's new! One traveled freely without passports. There was no income tax, no forced draft, no unemployment. An unwritten international law not only limited wars, but imposed truces. With universal agreement on the moral principles defining just wars and everything else, there was no need to define morality by statute. This international edifice was entirely the work of the Church, whose moral authority alone restrained political evils. To think that so splendid an economy could exist without the Church is arrant dementia.

The unity of Christendom was not the unity of mankind, but the unity of the Faith. God sent St. Joan to remind us that human governments may not be manipulated at pleasure without reference to the political order He has decreed. Whether wielded by democrats or despots, authority not conferred by Christ through His proper representatives, civil or ecclesiastical, is not lawful.

Where the state is separated from the Church, unity is destroyed at its very source; dissension and rebellion become ordinary conditions of existence. Civil society is parted from its very soul when it is deprived of the moral guidance God ordained for it. Church and state, like man and wife, soul and body, are one social unit. What God has joined together, man puts asunder at his peril (*Matt. 10:6*).

Continuing to spearhead the international utopia she envisioned in Joan of Arc's time, England has kept the world in turmoil by a consistent policy of "balance of power." It continues to be the guiding force behind the international Common Markets now in the process of formation. With economics as the new principle of unity, major political reorganization must follow. It is no accident that English has replaced Latin as the world's international language. Although now self-governing, America is still in many ways an English colony, especially its so-called "Eastern Establishment," which has never broken free of the financial and cultural ties binding it to its mother country. With a few minor exceptions, the foreign policy of the two nations is identical.

In 1991 the British monarch Elizabeth II not only knighted an American general, Norman Schwartzkopf, in recognition of services rendered in the Persian Gulf War, but for the first time in history openly addressed both houses of the American Congress. The date, May 16, is significant, for it is the anniversary of the canonization of Joan of Arc. Equally significant is the public admission made by the Queen on that historic occasion, reported by the Washington Post on the following day:

"Britain is at the heart of a growing movement towards greater cohesion within Europe," spelling "radical economic, social and political evolution." Her Majesty added:

> *It is Britain's prime concern to ensure that the new Europe is open and liberal and that it works in growing harmony with the United States and other members of the Atlantic community ... We must not allow ourselves to be enticed into a form of continental insularity.*

Carroll Quigley said as much in 1966 in *Tragedy and Hope*, where he noted, "There does exist ... an international Anglophile network ... which we may identify as the Round Table groups." It believes "that England was an Atlantic rather than a European power and must be allied, or federated, with the U.S ... It wishes to remain unknown."

Let us not assume that monarchy *per se* is incompatible with utopia. Henry V of England didn't find it so, and today's false constitutional monarchs, closely allied as they are to international money interests, would find it even less so. It is furthermore common knowledge that the British royal family supports syncretism. Global interfaith organizations with political overtones like Global Forum and the one launched by Prince Philip in 1989 are the very stuff of utopia.

Joan of Arc's battle with the English may therefore have only begun. There are many clues in her life which would lead to the conclusion that her mission to defend Christ's kingship was actually meant more for our day than it was for hers. Among the most striking is the fact that her Voices always addressed her as *"Jehanne la Pucelle, fille de Dieu."* (Joan the virgin, daughter of God.) It was as la Pucelle, the virgin, that Joan announced herself to the king, and she used the appellation six times in her letter to the English. Once her mission began, she was never known to identify herself in any other way. Her worst enemies at the University of Paris called her "that woman la Pucelle." Even her judge Bishop Cauchon cited her in court as "a woman by the name of Joan, commonly known as la Pucelle."

She is the only saint in the calendar known as "the virgin," a title heretofore reserved exclusively to the Mother of God. The Immaculate Virgin Mary, as Mother of the Son of God and His Mystical Body is preeminently the Virgin-Mother of the Church in the supernatural order. Joan was not a nun, nor did she have a religious vocation in the accepted sense. All due proportion kept, in view of the purely political nature of her mission, we must conclude that if heaven has indeed designated Joan as "the virgin," she is specifically so in the temporal order.

In God's dispensation, Joan may therefore prove to be virgin mother of the Christian state. Whereas the renewal of the Church is confided to our Lady, the renewal of civil society may well have been specially confided, within due limits, to our dear little Joan. The answer thus far remains with God. It's curious, however, that the French word *pucelle*, in ordinary use in that day, has survived only in connection with Joan. It would seem that once it had been applied to her, it died, was sanctified and mysteriously removed from the world's everyday vocabulary. Ironically enough, only its obsolete English equivalent, *puzzel*, has survived. Its meaning degenerated, however, into one designating a slut or a courtesan, the exact opposite of a virgin.

On the way to her very first meeting with Charles Joan prophesied that she would one day be the mother of a Pope, an Emperor, and a king, a cryptic utterance which was met at the time with derision and some rough jokes on the part of the soldiery. When she was asked to explain it, she replied that the time had not yet come, but that the Holy Ghost would see to it. Perhaps she was referring to the Great Monarch and the Great Pope whom, according to Scripture and so many saints and seers, God would raise up in the latter days. Nearly all the prophecies on the subject - and there are literally volumes of them - agree that the Monarch would be a saint of the Frankish royal line who would re-conquer the world for Christ under a Great Pope, also of Frankish royal descent, by whom he would eventually be constituted Emperor.

The abbot Merlin in particular prophesied that this Monarch would be the last king of England, which henceforth would be ruled by three lords appointed by him. This might distress Queen Elizabeth, implying as it does that England may not be a nation in her own right at all in the divine dispensation, but mayhap even a fief of France! It is strange that Joan once referred to her victory at Orleans and the crowning of Charles as "signs." Although in themselves major turning points in world history, these events may nonetheless have prefigured something much more decisive to follow. If the defeat of the English and the crowning of Charles were indeed signs of the future, they prefigure admirably the crowning of the Great Monarch who as King and Emperor will defeat the enemies of the divine social order and re-establish the reign of Christ the King.

We know from Joan's trial that she made certain revelations to the king which she refused to divulge. A month before her death she was subjected to a grueling interrogation in prison by her captors, who hoped to extract information concerning a mysterious sign she had given Charles. Joan would only answer, "It is beauteous and honorable, it is good and the richest in the world ... No man may describe anything so rich as this sign ... An angel from God and none other delivered the sign."

When they asked her whether it still existed, she replied, "It's good to know it will last a thousand years and more." "Then where is it?" she was asked. "The sign," she replied, "is in the King's treasury," and they could get no more out of her. Make of this what we will. We do know the satanic forces pitted against Joan were so powerful it took 500 years to canonize her. When this finally occurred on May 16, 1920, Cardinal Pie was of the opinion that "secret permanent relations were established between the Church Triumphant and the Church Militant."

Because canonization often seems to confer a kind of second mission on saints, sometimes more glorious than the first, many thought that raising Joan to the altars marked a new point of departure for her. After all, "The greatest deed ever accomplished for Christianity," in which she had invited the English to join her, has yet to be performed. We may confidently expect it, however, for even as she awaited execution in prison Joan promised visitors to her cell that eventually everything she came to do would be accomplished.

Jehanne la Pucelle saved Christendom once, and she can save it again. If the situation was desperate in her day, consider what it is in ours, when the last fragments of Christendom are disappearing into the maw of the man-made utopia! Yet save it she will, and when she does, we may expect her to do it the same way she did it the first time: She will begin by restoring the kingdom of France, and by God's grace, the rest of the nations will rise and follow France back to their Lord and ruler Jesus Christ. In a discourse to the French cardinals in 1911, St. Pius X predicted: "The nation which made an alliance with God at the baptismal fonts of Reims will repent and return to her first vocation."

The enemies of Christ the King tremble at the thought of the resurrection of Catholic France, principal defender of the Church and prime target of the enemy's occult forces. In 1878, on the occasion of Leo XIII's encyclical *Quod Apostolici muneris* warning of the dangers of socialism, the editors of a radical periodical called *The Revolution* stated the issue clearly: "The modem world is caught between the completion of the French Revolution and a return pure and simple to the Christianity of the middle ages!" No one knows better than Christ's enemies that there are no other options.

THE BEAST FROM THE SEA

At the site of the old Colonial capital in Williamsburg, Virginia, some portentous digging was recently undertaken in the old Bruton Parish churchyard. The secret writings of Francis Bacon, author of *The New Atlantis*, are supposed to have been buried there, and if they ever come to light, some sinister roots of American democracy may be exposed in the process. So far we possess only the first part of the Atlantis, an allegorical work on ideal government published a year after Bacon's death by his chaplain William Rawley.

It describes a mythical kingdom called Bensalem, a commonwealth of sages where an Order called the House of Salomon, or "the college of the six days' work" explores every branch of learning for the betterment of mankind. According to the brotherhood, "The end of our foundation is the knowledge of causes and secret motions of things; and the enlarging of the bounds of empire, to the effecting of all things possible." Seeking control of the universe through knowledge, their ultimate goal was that of the ancient alchemists: the perfection of man by his own efforts.

Some of the Order's inventions are made public, others are not. The people of Bensalem are of Jewish descent, whose laws are supposedly derived from a Mosaic *kabbala*. Their sages communicate with others worldwide through twelve "Merchants of Light" and a host of lesser officials, all under oaths of secrecy, who bring to Bensalem "the books and abstracts and patterns of experiments of all other parts."

The occultist writer Manly Palmer Hall maintained that it is common knowledge among the European secret societies that there exists a second part of *The New Atlantis*. This the diggers hoped to find among other arcane documents in the Bruton churchyard. Presumably it contains the laws and constitution of the ideal state, the real world government called "the commonwealth of the wise." That such a master plan lay behind the Constitution of the U.S. is within the bounds of possibility, for it is certain that our Constitution did not originate in America.

Political fantasies on ideal governments had long been fashionable in Europe, especially after the appearance of *The New Island of Utopia*, attributed to St. Thomas More. We say "attributed," for his imaginary republic, supposedly discovered by an associate of Amerigo Vespucci, is suspiciously Atlantean in inspiration. In no sense Christian, its government is based entirely on reason. All property is held in common, and freedom of religion is guaranteed, with divorce and euthanasia permitted.

If St. Thomas did write this work, he could only have meant it as satire. (Indeed some parts are quite funny, but readers interested in shaping the world seem inclined to take everything dead seriously.) It is suspicious, however, that the work was supposed to have been produced while More was on a diplomatic mission to the Low Countries in 1515. Published in Latin the following year, it appeared in English only in 1551, and from Holland, hotbead of humanism.

In 1623 Tommaso Campanella's *City of the Sun* made its contribution. James Harrington, the seventeenth century English political philosopher whose agrarian theories Thomas Jefferson so admired, seems to have been the first to have provided his version of ideal government with an actual constitution. His *Commonwealth of Oceana*, a rare copy of which can be viewed at the Folger Shakespearean Library in Washington, D.C., actually contains broad outlines of the future U.S. Constitution. Envisioning a republic based on property and guided by "wisdom," it features a bicameral legislature and the indirect election of the president. Figuring prominently therein is the allegedly unique American system of checks and balances between three executive, legislative and judicial arms of government.

+

According to Hall, "it was Bacon's dream that the college of the six days should be erected in America," which with good reason he identified with Atlantis. It was commonly believed in classical times that that great island continent had lain just off America's east coast. When it sank, taking its sophisticated civilization with it to the bottom of the sea, a nearly impenetrable barrier of silt and seaweed formed over the waters, literally cutting America off from the rest of the world. Columbus, a learned and experienced navigator, would have "discovered" it at the precise time the barrier had subsided sufficiently for a large ship to sail through.

At the time of the catastrophe, many Atlanteans must have fled to the mainland, or perhaps had been left stranded there, for there had been close ties between the north American coast and the island. Their descendants would become the region's so-called Indian tribes, particularly the Iroquois, whose unusually developed political organization has never been adequately explained, and which could hardly have arisen spontaneously. In the annals of the French missionaries to the region are found many references to the particularly satanic nature of some of those adjoining native cultures. One tribe to the north they actually named "the Sorcerers."

The famous Iroquois League, a federal union of five (and later six) nations which according to oral tradition dated as far back as 1000 A.D., had an unwritten constitution based on principles disturbingly similar to our own. Authority resided in the people, whose leaders were regarded as public servants; the people possessed the right of recall of their elected representatives; woman suffrage was accepted on principle; and most important of all, any and all religions were tolerated.

Benjamin Franklin is said to have used the Iroquois League as the model for his first proposed "Albany Plan" to unite the English Colonies for mutual defense against the French. The slogan for the plan was "Unite or Die," accompanied by a picture of a fractured snake whose pieces must be put together to form a whole. The snake in question was no ordinary one. It was the Ouroboros, a serpent well-known to alchemists. Usually represented with its tail in its mouth, it is an ancient symbol of that self-government and ultimate self-perfection to which the sages of Bensalem were dedicated. American democracy may therefore owe more to the somber ideals of Atlantis than is generally suspected.

According to Manly Hall in *The Secret Destiny of America*:

Bacon's secret society was set up in America before the middle of the 17th century. Bacon himself had given up all hope of bringing his dream to fruition in his own country, and he concentrated his attention upon rooting it in the new world. He made sure that the American colonists were thoroughly indoctrinated with the principles of religious tolerance, political democracy and social equality. Through carefully appointed representatives, the machinery of democracy was set up at least a hundred years before the period of the

*Revolutionary War ... Bacon's secret society membership was
not limited to England ...*

*The Alchemists, Cabalists, Mystics and Rosicrucians were
the incisive instruments ... Representatives of these groups
migrated to the colonies at an early date and set up their
organization in suitable places. These American organizations
were branches under European sovereignty, with the members
in the two hemispheres bound together with the strongest bonds
of sympathy and understanding ... Historians have never
ceased to wonder at the enormous psychological influence
which Franklin exercised in colonial politics ... Franklin was
not a lawmaker, but as the appointed spokesman of the
unknown philosophers, his words became law.*

+

Unlike God, man is not self-sufficient. Not only is he dependent
on his Creator, but he requires the cooperation of his kind to supply
his needs, one of the most insistent of which is to be governed by
other men. Wherever he becomes estranged from God, he
inevitably succumbs to some ideal government of his own making,
for the devil, ever desirous of displacing God's order with his own,
puts his preternatural cunning only too readily at the service of
human intelligence. He specializes in utopias, whose construction is
merely an expression in political terms of his primordial *non
serviam*.

Although Francis Bacon is generally credited with originating
modern Masonry, and Benjamin Franklin with discovering
electricity, neither of them invented Utopia. They merely ushered in
the modern stage of the long occult tradition which began with the
world's first artificial cities built by Cain and the men of Babel and
which has never died out. Wherever men settled they took with
them the same old perverted craving for self-government which
they had inherited from their ancestors, but after Babel they were
restrained in their ambitions by the differences in race and language
which God had imposed on mankind, so that henceforth they could
be allowed to govern themselves more or less according to the
normal dictates of reason.

Over the centuries nation after nation rose and fell, swallowed
up by empire upon empire following the course of nature. These

mighty political agglomerates were shown in a dream to Nebuchadnezzar, King of Babylon, under the aspect of a great statue whose head "was of fine gold, but the breast and the arms of silver, and the belly and the thighs of brass: And the legs of iron, the feet part of iron and part of clay." (*Dan. 2:32-3*). As governments they were far from perfect, but the dark penchant for independent rule, inherited from the devil through Cain, was not a first principle. None could have been considered utopian, for in no sense were they idealized constructions put together out of whole cloth. Certainly none operated from abstract principles determined be forehand, into which society had to be arbitrarily fitted. Even Plato's Republic never spilled from manuscript into practice.

For the most part they grew organically, rising and falling with the normal interplay of forces both good and bad. The vast majority were monarchies functioning in accordance with natural law. The abstract notion that all men are created equal would have met with derision in Nineveh or Babylon and indeed even in Athens. Although giving official worship to the true God only now and then, as did Nebuchadnezzar, all would nonetheless have repudiated separation of church and state as farcical. Every empire had a state religion, whose gods were venerated as a civic duty. Supernatural reality was never denied on principle. The same could be said generally of all pagan peoples at all times.

+

The resurgence of the great satanic utopia, a political monster subsisting on its own without reference to God or the supernatural, is a phenomenon of the latter times. Standing upon the sand of the sea, St. John in the visions of Patmos saw this apocalyptic beast:

> *... coming up out of the sea, having seven heads and ten horns, and upon his horns ten diadems, and upon his heads names of blasphemy ...*
>
> *And the dragon (figure of the devil) gave him his own strength and great power ... And it was given unto him to make war with the saints, and to overcome them. And power was given him over every tribe and tongue and nation"* (*Apo. 13:1,7*).

This first beast is a composite political power, whose function is to prepare the way for a second beast, a false ecclesiastical power pictured in the Apocalypse as a lamb speaking with the very voice of the dragon, in other words, the satanic church in sheep's clothing.

After centuries of underground preparation, the first beast did literally rise from the sea, sending out its first surreptitious tentacles from England, that unfortunate island kingdom once known as "our Lady's Bower," but which was the first to fall to the Reformation. If we are to credit the internal testimony of *The New Atlantis*, from that point on the revolution was disseminated in Europe largely by Sephardic Jews acting through secret societies organized along the lines described by Bacon. The way to the new world was prepared by John Dee, that infamous practitioner of the black arts with international connections in high places who gained a fateful ascendancy over Queen Elizabeth. Coining the phrase "British Empire" before there was one, Dee successfully promoted English settlement in Catholic America in defiance of papal authority and existing international law. Playing on the unfortunate rivalries of France and Spain, the upstart colonies not only held their ground, but ended by taking root. Out of them would emerge the United States of America. Many utopias had existed on paper, but now the *Novus Ordo Seclorum* actually began to materialize, and "all the earth was in admiration of the beast." (*Apo. 13:3*)

It should be clear by now that the United States was never conceived "under God" in the light of Christian principles. Political emancipation from God and His Vicar on earth lay at the very heart of the newly hatched secular utopia. In 1796, in the treaty with Tripoli, George Washington would formally declare, "the government of the United States is not in any sense founded on the Christian religion." Despite the fact that its population was predominately Christian, as a political entity it was unequivocally "conceived in liberty and dedicated to the proposition that all men are created equal," just as Abraham Lincoln said at Gettysburg. This was a first among Christian nations.

The mere motion to open the Constitutional Convention with a prayer, artfully made by Benjamin Franklin, had been vociferously voted down. Nowhere in the text of the Constitution does the name of God occur, not even the vague Deist God of the Founding Fathers who figures in the Declaration of Independence. One looks in vain through the Federalist Papers or similar revolutionary writings for biblical allusions. Where there are any, they are often blasphemous, as in Thomas Paine's well-known *Age of Reason*.

Until the 1930's history books hardly mentioned any ecclesiastical influences in the shaping of the United States. Religion was certainly tolerated, even encouraged for political ends as a force contributing powerfully to public order, but its status was always private, strictly limited to individuals or religious bodies existing apart from the body politic. In the new Utopia, no magisterium but its own Supreme Court had any legal standing. The Holy Catholic Church, founded by the Son of God for the salvation and social regulation of mankind, had to work in this context or not at all, and even then humbly to take its place as just one denomination among others.

In 1789, the memorable year which saw the ratification of the U.S. Constitution and the outbreak of the French Revolution, the first institution of higher learning without religious affiliation ever seen among Christians was chartered in the United States. No courses whatever in religion figured in its curriculum. It was the University of Virginia, brainchild of Thomas Jefferson, whose view of revealed religion comes clear in his so-called "Jefferson Bible," a version of Scripture for reasonable men from which he had expurgated all supernatural content. Fearing to ruin himself politically by offending his Christian contemporaries, he forbade its publication during his lifetime. It made no public appearance until 1902, and then only in a limited edition. Since the Second Vatican Council it has become readily available.

Unlike that of any other nation, the Great Seal of the United States is two-faced, with an obverse and a reverse, like a medal. Its secret underside was concealed until the twentieth century when, during the administration of Brother Franklin Delano Roosevelt, it suddenly appeared on the national currency. On the one dollar bill, crowning an uncompleted "pyramid of progress" may be read the words, *Annuit coeptis*. In other words, the United States from the beginning was only a beginning. Already back in 1787 Benjamin Rush could see, "The American War is over, but this is far from the case of the American Revolution. On the contrary, nothing but the first act of the great drama is over."

An apostolate to free the rest of the world from the constraints of religion still lay ahead. The first political entity to operate successfully from a written constitution the United States bore no resemblance to those governments which had existed before Christendom, for it was put together not by pagans, but by Christians acting under occult direction with a special purpose in mind. From its inception it had been set up in formal disregard of Christ the King, to whom all power in heaven and on earth had been given. Once firmly rooted, it succeeded in driving entirely from the North American continent the two great Catholic powers in legal possession.

Gradually it would win to its cause the whole of the vast hemisphere claimed for Christ by Columbus, which Catholic saints and martyrs had explored, colonized, evangelized, and watered with their blood. As a consequence the Faith, which was winning souls by the millions after the appearance of Our Lady of Guadalupe on American soil, would be subjected to unremitting persecution. Quietly and with relatively little violence, it would be systematically decimated in the name of democracy and religious liberty. In the United States it would be "tolerated" to death, in a climate of ecumenism characterized by an annual Thanksgiving Day, a special Thursday set apart on which everyone was encouraged to thank the god of his choice for his blessings.

+

As it turned out, the national ecumenism would be immeasurably furthered by Catholic citizens who, in their enthusiasm for the material benefits of the secular state, would develop a flourishing heresy for themselves. Aptly labeled *Americanism* by Pope Leo XIII, it would end by injecting the norms and ideals of utopia directly into the Church, not only in America, but wherever she was found in the world. Some may believe that Americanism is a product of Puritanism, but this is not the case. The two heresies do have some common ancestry, but one does not spring from the other. Like Calvin and Hobbes, they are distant cousins at best, not parent and child, with the heresy far more indebted to Thomas Hobbes than ever it was to John Calvin.

Americanism did not spring from Protestants, but from Catholics who arrived in the Colonies from England and Ireland under the highly equivocal leadership of Lord Baltimore. Their first attempt to found an ecumenical Catholic colony in Newfoundland having proved unsuccessful, they finally settled permanently in

Maryland, whence the virus spread nationwide via an establishment hierarchy. Strong promoters of the Revolution like their elected Bishop John Carroll, who owed his office to the personal endorsement of Benjamin Franklin, Americanist prelates maintained a stranglehold on the Catholic enclaves from the beginning through close ties with the functionaries of government.

Certainly Puritanism was a factor in the growth of Americanism, but only peripherally and superficially, by way of a shared culture and the general ambience. No doubt Puritanism can be blamed for much of the Protestant mentality that is prevalent among American Catholics. (As the canny Scot Hamish Fraser once put it, U.S. Catholics are Protestants who go to Mass.) Even so, its influence hardly ever extended farther than the nation's east coast.

Actually there are wide divergences between Puritanism and Americanism. To name only one instance, the Puritans displayed a positive aversion to ecumenism, which is a characteristic Americanist feature. Nor were Puritans noted for their missionary zeal, particularly towards the Indians, whom most evangelical divines considered hopeless prospects, degenerate beyond recall. Americanists, on the other hand, were fired with zeal, believing it their manifest destiny to convert not only all of America, but the entire world to their own inspired brand of democratic, watered down Catholicism.

When the Mother of God made her spectacular appearance on America's soil in 1531 - perhaps just as Francis Bacon was putting the finishing touches to *The New Atlantis* - she identified herself to the Indian convert Juan Diego as "the All-Perfect, the Destroyer of the Serpent." Transliterated from the Aztec language into "Our Lady of Guadalupe," this title was the one which the Pope would one day choose under which to declare her Patroness of all the Americas. Eschewing any explicit reference to the unprecedented apparition, first of the Marian interventions in modern times, the American Catholic hierarchy nonetheless voted at its First Plenary Council in Baltimore in 1846 to place the United States under the protection of the Immaculate Conception.

One would have thought that the Catholic faithful, who among all the citizens of the new republic should have had God's glory most at heart, would have been urged to campaign for an amendment to the Constitution formally acknowledging God's glory most at heart, would have been urged to campaign for an amendment to the Constitution formally acknowledging God's sovereignty over the nation. There is, alas, no serious evidence of any more having been made in so radical or so dangerous a direction

"They adored the beast, saying: Who is like to the beast? And who shall be able to fight with him?" (*Apo. 13:4*). By the time the Third Plenary Council met in 1884, the Catholic hierarchy under its first Cardinal James Gibbons solemnly declared that the nation's heroes were in fact the instruments used by God himself to make a home here for liberty. If the first beast of the Apocalypse took flesh in the United States, so did the second, for its outline could be clearly discerned in Americanism.

+

Its own Revolution won and consolidated, the United States lost no time in pursuing its apostolate to the world at large. Before long it would produce progeny in its own image by offering a workable blueprint to other nations still languishing under the outmoded laws of Christendom. Not that any other nation has ever actually used the U.S. Constitution as a model, for it was specifically English in its details and suited to special circumstances; but the secular principles on which it was drawn have taken over the world, and since the Second Vatican Council, by way of a novel "collegiality," they have seeped into the Church.

First target of the new messianism was France, for on her monarch, by divine dispensation "Christ's lieutenant in the temporal order," the Christian world order rested. If she fell, all Christendom would eventually fall with her, as indeed proved the case. Preparing the fall of France was therefore a real, if undeclared purpose of the American Revolution, as it had been that of the English. One usually thinks of the French Revolution as the first of the modern revolts against Christendom, but actually the American one was successfully concluded before the French even began.

True, the French Revolution was better calculated to capture the popular fancy. How could the Boston Tea Party hope to compete with the storming of the Bastille? But that is because in France there was fierce resistance on the part of a Catholic people. When their beloved King Louis XVI was decapitated by the guillotine, all Christendom lost its head.

The American Revolution, on the other hand, was accomplished with relative ease by a well-trained active minority of wealthy men with a long clandestine apprenticeship. The English sovereign had already been killed years before in the mother country, and in the colonies there was no established church to abolish. After Yorktown, the dust settled comparatively quickly, for thousands of loyal Englishmen who opposed the Revolution - among them a whole regiment composed entirely of Catholics - left millions in confiscated property behind them and fled back to England or to their compatriots in Canada, causing no further trouble.

Although the French Revolution killed many more people, in proportion to the population the American created five times as many exiles. Few people realize that the American Revolution was actually a *coup d'etat* directed against Christ the King, perpetrated against a Christian majority more absorbed in putting down roots than in revolting against their sovereign. Mostly transplanted workers with no aristocracy to defend them, and possessing no unity of faith, they were incapable of organized resistance and were easy prey to clever propaganda appealing to their lowest interests.

If nothing else, the American Revolution provided the French with an invaluable dress rehearsal. As the new American ambassador, Thomas Jefferson became the mentor of the worst Paris radicals literally overnight. It was Benjamin Franklin who introduced Voltaire into the Masonic Lodge of the Nine Muses in Paris, and not the other way round. Voltaire, Rousseau and the Encyclopedists, generally credited with fomenting the French Revolution, made no secret of the fact that they had culled their ideas from English revolutionaries like Bacon's secretary Thomas Hobbes, John Locke, Isaac Newton, Elias Ashmole and Desaguliers. Bacon himself Voltaire characterized as "the greatest of all philosophers."

Like Newton, most of these Englishmen were secret alchemists, dedicated to the ideals of the "college of the six days' work." Through their efforts and those of the secret societies, the entire intellectual climate of Europe was charged with the dazzling new Atlantean dream. As might be expected, highborn revolutionaries from Masonic lodges all over Europe rushed to help the American cause, men like the Marquis de la Fayette, Count de Rochambeau, Count de Grasse, Kosciuszko, Count Pulaski, de

Kalb and Baron von Steuben, not to mention a useful contingent of English-hating Irish.

Some of these officers, like Pulaski, openly brandished Masonic battle flags in the field. Thirty-three of General Washington's generals were Masons. Their exemplary loyalty in the face of his military incompetence is easily explained by their Masonic oaths, which would have spelled death for them had they dared break them. The Marquis de la Fayette tells us that Washington entrusted no serious duties to him until he had been inducted into Masonry.

Meanwhile, across the Atlantic, attention was kept riveted on developments in America by a press manipulated by Benjamin Franklin. A bogus American newspaper printed in Holland was circulated in Europe which released news specially calculated to win support for the cause. All Franklin's mail from abroad was routed through St. Eustasius, a Dutch owned island east of Puerto Rico where wealthy Sephardic Jews had established an opulent world trade center. Known as the Golden Rock, the island was a fulcrum for the American Revolution from the beginning, providing a lifeline of arms and ammunition and a base for espionage until it was destroyed by the British in 1781.

+

As Manly Hall would put it, "The rise of American democracy was necessary to a world program. At the appointed hour, the freedom of man was publicly declared." Every smoldering enemy of Christ the King was fired with hope by the American Revolution, for a handful of English colonials had finally proved that a man-made secular state based entirely on natural principles could be successfully set up in open defiance of the Catholic faith or any religious affiliation. Written constitutions began popping up everywhere, for the age of artificial nations was underway.

The whole world is now in the process of being dismembered and reassembled in the utopian image in accordance with the old alchemical adage so dear to Masonry, *Solve et coagula*, "dissolve and consolidate." World War II saw the creation of the present United Nations and the creation of enough new third world countries to throw mapmakers into despair. Efforts to put together a United States of Europe have long been underway. In 1947 the state of Israel, unique among artificial nations, was constituted in the Holy Land. After a bloody war its Knesset now sits in Jerusalem, which our Lord himself referred to as "the city of the great King" (*Matt.5:35*), and over which He wept.

+

The great satanic world republic was shown to the prophet Daniel under the figure of a beast "terrible and exceeding strong ... which shall be greater than all the kingdoms and shall devour the whole earth and shall tread down and break it in pieces" (*Dan. 7:7,23*). By its agency the demons which had been expelled by the coming of the Son of God would reinhabit the earth:

> *When an unclean spirit is gone out of a man he walks through dry places seeking rest and finds none. Then he says: I will return into my house from whence I came out. And coming he finds it empty, swept and garnished. Then he goes and takes with him seven other spirits more wicked than himself, and they enter in and dwell there: and the last state of that man is made worse than the first. So shall it be also to this wicked generation ... The men of Nineveh shall rise in judgment with this generation and shall condemn it (Matt. 12:43-45, 41).*

Our Lady told us at La Salette that the demonic hegemony could be expected to begin after 1864, when "Lucifer, together with a great number of devils will be loosed from hell." Because of neglect of prayer and penance among the leaders of God's people, "God will permit the ancient serpent to sow divisions among rulers, in all societies and in all families." The Apocalypse in fact tells us that the utopian beast would receive from the devil "his own strength and great power" and that men would adore him who bestowed this power (*Apo. 13:2,4*).

Although clearly prefigured from the beginning by Cain's city and again by the experiment at Babel, the utopian beast is a phenomenon of the Christian era. It would have been impossible for it to take final shape before the appearance of Christendom, because essentially it is a mirror-image, international like Christendom and extending to "every tribe and people and tongue and nation" (*Apo. 13:7*). Having no existence apart from the Church, for centuries it could only fester silently in Her shadow against the day when the sins of men allowed it sufficient stature to challenge Her authority. It did not, could not arise among the heathen of King Nebuchadnezzar's day, but only among Christians.

The king's dream of the symbolic statue, portraying the old governments of the world, had ended abruptly. He saw the idol suddenly shattered to dust by a mysterious stone, "cut out of a mountain without hands," whereupon "the stone that struck the statue became a great mountain and filled the whole earth." Thus was he given to understand that God would one day intervene again in human politics in some unforeseen manner. This time, Daniel told him, He would do so by establishing "a kingdom that shall never be destroyed," which "shall break in pieces and consume all these kingdoms and itself shall stand forever" (*Dan. 2:34-5,44*).

And so it happened. At the height of the Roman Empire, the last of the ancient world governments, prefigured by the feet of the statue, during an interlude of unprecedented peace, God entered history as one of the Empire's least subjects. Without any warning to the general public, He was born to a royal Virgin named Mary in Bethlehem, the city of David, where His parents had come to comply with an imperial decree "that the whole world should be enrolled" (*Luke 2:1*).

As Jesus Christ the King, God himself had come to earth at last to lay the foundations, as it were, of His own Utopia. This was the Holy Catholic Church, the only perfect society the world could ever know. Put to death for His efforts by those who "hated him," and "will not have this man to rule over us" (*Luke 19:14*), He rose from the tomb and ascended to heaven, whence He reigns in majesty as King of kings at the right hand of the Father.

His first royal act on His accession was to send the Holy Ghost to animate and inform His new government among men: At the close of Pentecost, when all "were persevering with one mind in prayer with the women and Mary the mother of Jesus and with all his brethren" (*Acts 1:14*), the calamity which had occurred at Babel was reversed: "They began to speak in divers tongues, according as the Holy Ghost gave them to speak," while at the same time, "out of every nation under heaven ... every man heard him speak in his own tongue" (*Acts 2:46*).

The divine Utopia, the "city with fixed foundations whose builder and maker is God" (*Heb. 11:10*), against which the gates of hell could never prevail, was officially inaugurated. It would be, writes Fr. Juan Arintero in *The Mystical Evolution*:

> *The vastest, most complex, and in every way the most admirable of living organisms. As the mystical society of all the Christian faithful, it enjoys a real and true life and not merely a moral life as do merely human societies, because it has Jesus Christ as its Head and His divine Spirit as its soul ...*

All men are not created equal:

> *Since organization presupposes inequality, diversity of elements and subordination, the perfection of an organism does not consist in the perfection of one member, however noble it may be, nor in various equivalent members, but in the harmonious combination of many members of unequal nobility and of diverse functions.*

Politics has never been the same since this supernatural agency for the regulation of man's social relations with God and his fellow men was established in the world. Hereafter any political arrangement put together without its cooperation, ignoring the supernatural on principle, would be at odds with reality. With that first Pentecost, any man-made utopia became truly utopian, chimerical and impractical in the most ordinary sense of that word.

Now more than ever, "Unless the Lord build the house, they labor in vain that build it" (*Ps. 126:1*). Constitutional amendments and executive orders notwithstanding, God himself has told us, "Without Me you can do nothing." Pope St. Pius X put it plainly in his letter to the Sillon: "The state cannot be built unless the Church lays the foundations and supervises the work." We who are now witnessing the continuing alchemical transformation of the United States of America into "something rich and strange" can rely on the truth of his words: "You cannot build a society without God."

He hurled at utopian planners a resounding:

> *NO! Civilization does not have to be invented, nor the New City built in the clouds. It already has been; it is here! It is Christian civilization, the Catholic City. The only problem is to keep setting it up and restoring it on its natural foundations*

*against the ever-recurring attacks of the unhealthy utopia of
revolt and impiety!*

Utopians are in for a sad disappointment if they think their ideal
government can be anything but a police state. At La Salette our
Lady repeated nearly word for word the warning delivered in St.
John's Apocalypse when she told the child Mélanie Calvat,
"Society is on the eve of the most terrible scourges and the greatest
events; you must expect to be governed by a rod of iron and to drink
the chalice of God's wrath."

She promised that eventually God would intervene once more
on earth, but this time it would be by striking "in an unparalleled
manner." This time, "water and fire will purify the earth and
consume all the works of men's pride, and everything will be
renewed. God will be served and glorified." Before that happens,
however, "God will abandon men to themselves." What
punishment could better fit the crime of godless self-government
than being abandoned in Utopia? Abandoned in a place whose
name means "Nowhere ?"Thank God, as Pius X said, the Church is
always "Here."

THE USURPERS

To most Americans the word "politics" means "voting." For over two hundred years we have been conditioned to view the fine art of politics as little more than the skillful manipulation of yeas and nays in an arena where someone is always running for election and some new policy being considered. There seems to be no other way, for according to our Declaration of Independence all men are created equal. Furthermore, because governments:

> *... derive their just powers from the consent of the governed ... it is the right of the people to alter or to abolish ... and to institute a new government, laying its foundations on such principles, and organizing its powers in such form as to them shall seem most likely to effect their safety and happiness.*

This revolutionary doctrine established perpetual change as principle. In a political economy where men are all equal and must govern themselves as they see fit at any given moment, obviously some means of arriving at a consensus must be devised. So far, voting has provided the only practical solution to the problem. It was the expedient agreed upon for making one out of many and getting something done. Without voting, the national *pluribus* would have no *unum* worth mentioning. It is the indispensable building-block of democracy and inalienable warrant of individual liberty.

Catholics should know better, but probably can't if they were cradled in the democratic religion. In the beginnings of the republic, the first three American bishops were actually nominated and elected by vote of the clergy in what was hailed at the time as a happy accommodation to the democratic process on the Church's part. These were John Carroll and his two coadjutors, Lawrence Graessl and Leonard Neale, Carroll's successor to the See of Baltimore. Carroll was elected in 1789 at Whitemarsh, Maryland, by the 24 priests of Maryland and Pennsylvania. Neale and Graessl were elected within the next decade. Already plans had been laid for holding a national Catholic council, and it was hoped that eventually the laity would be allowed some part in the government of their new American Church.

Fortunately Rome permitted these first elections only as an exception, *pro prima hac vice tantum*, and soon put a stop to them. Otherwise, episcopal election campaigns similar to those of our civil officials might well have become part of Catholic life early on in the new republic. They may yet, for the Second Vatican Council's decree *Gaudium et Spes* has brought us so unprecedented an endorsement of the whole democratic *apparat* as would have rejoiced any Americanist's heart:

> *It is in full accord with human nature that juridical-political structures should, with ever better success and without any discrimination, afford all their citizens the chance to participate freely and actively in establishing the constitutional bases of a political community, governing the state, determining the scope and purpose of various institutions, and choosing leaders. Hence let all citizens be mindful of their simultaneous right and duty to vote freely in the interest of advancing the common good.*

In the Abbott translation of this revolutionary document a footnote occurs here which calls attention, if somewhat obliquely, to the Council's departure from tradition:

> *This passage stresses ... the full compatibility of maximal representative government with the dignity of the human person. Here is clearly an advance from the suspicions of democracy that found favor in so many areas of Catholic thought throughout the nineteenth and the present century.*

Suspicions strongly voiced, we might add, and culminating in open condemnations on the part of Popes from Pius VI on down. Never before has the Church formally promoted the appanage of modern democracy or designated voting as a Christian duty. If "the Spirit of Vatican II" ever brings general elections within the Church at large as it has among the bishops, simple voting may be expected to discharge all those subtle functions heretofore reserved to the Holy Ghost. Voting will usher in all the paraphernalia geared to raising those mighty gusts of public opinion which can be counted on to propel the bark of Peter as they do our ship of state.

Sail on! That wily politician Abraham Lincoln would have scoffed at the idea, as did George Washington, that the U.S. was founded on Christian principles. Under no illusions regarding the springs of democratic power, he declared without subterfuge, "Our government rests on public opinion. Whoever can change public opinion can change the government practically as such." In other words, in a democracy, whoever can change public opinion can control votes.

Although votes may be integral to democracy, the faith alone should tell us they are not integral to politics. The connection is entirely accidental. Human government draws its fundamentals from natural law, which does not change with the times. Opinion has nothing to do with it. Universal suffrage, now accepted as a law of life, was an eighteenth century innovation, unknown till then even in the Greek city states. For thousands of years great empires subsisted without it.

Until the Second Vatican Council imposed the blessings of collegiality on Catholic bishops, the Holy Roman Catholic Church, the only perfect society ever to arise among men, had functioned flawlessly without ever subjecting any of her deliberations to a vote. This does not mean she had no use for voting as such. The Church normally votes when her cardinals elect a Pope, although even that is not absolutely necessary. Should the dying pontiff prefer to appoint his successor, he may do so. Superiors of religious communities are likewise ordinarily elected by their members, but here too they may be appointed by a higher authority.

By making provision for limited voting, the Church has preserved subsidiarity, a principle which forms part of her very nature. Briefly, subsidiarity means that underlings must be allowed as much autonomy as consistent with their position in the hierarchy of government. This is true particularly of bishops in their own sees. No central authority may usurp the privileges and duties of a lower echelon, nor can these cast their responsibilities on those above. Where subsidiarity is respected, neither the welfare mentality nor despotism can thrive.

Yves Dupont writes, "Subsidiarity, to be sure, does not exclude supreme authority, or arbitration, but it is undoubtedly the antithesis of autocratism. The word itself is comparatively new, but the principle has always been upheld by the Church." Even the U.S. Constitution acknowledged subsidiarity in principle when it adopted the Bill of Rights in 1791. Article IX reads, "The enumeration in the Constitution, of certain rights, shall not be construed to deny or disparage others retained by the people." Article IX reads "The enumeration in the Constitution, of certain rights, shall not be construed to deny or disparage others retained by the people." Article X reads, "The powers not delegated to the United States by the Constitution, nor prohibited by it to the States, are reserved to the States respectively, or to the people."

After the death blow dealt to states' rights by the Civil War, these articles gradually became dead letters, with the results we see today. Left to itself, unrestricted universal suffrage cannot prevent the central government from usurping rights at all levels of government, even down to that of the family. Sooner or later the citizen must look to "the government" to regulate and supply nearly everything. With subsidiarity gone, democracy inevitably devolves into totalitarianism.

What voting takes place in the Church has so far always been within, and subject to, her basic political structure, which is strictly monarchical. It has often been said that in the middle ages, when all governments operated in like fashion, there was more real democracy in the world than there is today. According to Dupont:

> *True, there have been autocratic monarchs in the long history of Christendom, but these monarchs were not really Catholic in the true sense of the word, and even many of the so-called autocratic monarchs were much more liberal - in the true sense of the word - than the liberals who have instituted democracy with its all- encompassing bureaucracy.*

He goes on to say,

> *I recently read a book that gave extensive quotations from original documents which have been preserved in most French town halls in towns and villages. The remarkable thing about these documents was the tone as well as the contents. They were written during the reign of Louis XIV, the most autocratic of the French kings. Yet those in authority spoke to their subjects in a friendly and father-like manner, and with the utmost courtesy.*

None of the 'First and Final Notice' or 'Take notice that ...' or again, 'You are hereby directed to ... ' and so forth, in the bureaucratic manner so familiar to us.

The subjects were addressed as 'My dear ... 'and they were 'requested to be so kind as to ... ,' because 'I would be extremely grateful if you would kindly consider this matter,' and the closing sentence from the Governor, the Magistrate or the landlord was to draw 'the blessing of God upon you and your family.' All the documents were in the same vein; they were written from person to person, not from a nameless and faceless bureaucracy to an equally nameless and faceless mass of 'citizens.' ... As regards the contents, the documents in question made it obvious that the powers of the 'Law' were limited. There was no threat of penalty 'for failure to comply,' no 'fine or 3 months in jail' as we currently see in our official documents.

The Masons, agnostics and atheists who are responsible for the rise of democracy must, of course, perpetuate the myth that monarchy means autocratism. Autocratism presupposes centralization of powers; the hierarchical structure of a Christian monarchy is just the opposite, each having certain powers according to his rank in the hierarchy, and each region, province, city, town and village enjoying a measure of genuine democracy - (the smaller the social unit, the greater that measure is) - as taught by St. Thomas Aquinas and, again, by Pius XII.

+

The essence of politics is not votes, but the transmission of authority, which according to natural law can only proceed downward from God throughout society. So the Church always taught before the Second Vatican Council. Voting as practiced in modern times is the indispensable adjunct to the democratic heresy because it is the device whereby authority is allegedly transmitted upward from the people instead of downward from God.

Writes Dupont:

It is also Church teaching, that authority, that is, God's authority, cannot rise from the people for the simple reason that God's authority is not vested in the people." He notes further that this "was confirmed by Leo XIII in Graves communi *and again by St. Pius X in* Notre Charge Apostolique. *The common source is, of course, the Summa Theologica of St. Thomas Aquinas. We all know that this teaching is currently disregarded in the Conciliarist Church (which is the Church of Man and Democracy).*

Because all authority flows downward from one source, which is God, the very order of reality binds authority indissolubly to monarchy.

Even in a democracy, to exercise authority at all, sooner or later some one person, or persons acting as one, must command the others. This poses a perpetual dilemma for democracy, whose apparent rule from below is never more than magical illusion. In these latter days, the political prestidigitation called democratic voting may rank among those "signs and wonders, to seduce (if it were possible) even the elect" (*Mark 13:22*), for its powers of seduction have proved enormous.

Democracy would have us believe that it has eliminated the monarch whereas in fact it has only displaced him. It should be obvious that monarchy has in no way been abolished by driving kings and emperors from their thrones. Anyone who says kings have been exterminated simply doesn't know what has been going on for the last 200 years. The truth is they have proliferated all over the earth, to the point that now we don't even notice them. Voting has become indispensable where every man is a king, or has been persuaded that he can become one if he sets his mind to it.

Because it is impossible to do away with monarchy without doing away with authority altogether, monarchy was perforce usurped by the people. The substitution was clearly seen at the time by Tories like the dour colonial who remarked regarding George III that he'd rather have one tyrant across the sea than thousands of them here at home. Where one man sat in majesty as personal embodiment of the nation, every person in the nation now squabbles for a seat. In *Le Saint Pape et le Grand Monarque, de la Franquerie* tells of an apparition recorded in a dossier put together with a view to the canonization of Louis XVI in which the martyred

King is alleged to have said, "Many have seated themselves on my throne to their own destruction!"

Our Lord told the politician Pilate, "*Rex sum Ego*, I am a king" (*John 18:37*). Or, as a more literal translation of the Vulgate would support, "I am King." Ultimately, to wish to rid oneself of monarchy is to wish to rid oneself of God, to usurp the monarchy of God. If we read history correctly, this is precisely what modern democracy set itself to do.

+

The powers of Christian monarchy, derived from God's own and patterned on the Gospels, were parceled out among the people, "that it might be fulfilled which was spoken by the prophet, saying, They divided my garments among them; and upon my vesture they cast lots" (*Matt. 27:35*). Donning the garments of the king for the first time in 1776, those who "will not have this man to reign over us" (*Luke 19:14*), proclaimed in their own name, "*Rex sumus*. We are king!"

A proof of record is the U. S. Constitution. When it solemnly set up the first man-made modern democracy, it was composed of three interdependent branches - executive, legislative and judicial. These powers which democracy arrogated to itself pertain specifically to royalty. By formal declaration the Constitution usurped the three functions whose source is found in the person of the king.

No matter that the people are incapable of conferring such powers, on the king or on anyone else. Yet the fact remains that they can be delegated only by the three divine Persons of the triune God, through the mediation of Christ, who said even as He ascended to His throne on high, "All power is given to me in heaven and in earth" (*Matt, 28:18*). It is precisely in terms of these three royal powers that Pius XI chose to define the lordship of Christ in the encyclical Quas primas:

His kingship consists, says the Pope:

> *... in a threefold power which is essential to lordship. This is sufficiently clear from ... scriptural testimony ... concerning the universal dominion of our Redeemer, and moreover it is a dogma of faith that Jesus Christ was given to man, not only as*

*our Redeemer, but also as a lawgiver, to whom obedience is
due. Not only do the Gospels tell us that He made laws, but they
present Him to us in the act of making them. Those who keep
them show their love for their divine Master, and He promises
that they shall remain in His love.*

*He claimed judicial power as received from His Father,
when the Jews accused Him of breaking the Sabbath by the
miraculous cure of a sick man. 'For neither doth the Father
judge any man; but hath given all judgment to the Son.' In this
power is included the right of rewarding and punishing all men
living, for this right is inseparable from that of judging.
Executive power, too, belongs to Christ, for all must obey His
commands; none may escape them, nor the sanctions He
imposed.*

Needless to say, although democracy vested itself in the
garments of royalty, it could never play convincingly the role of the
true monarchy it had supplanted. In its greed for power, it assumed
in democratic form monarchy's deadly counterfeit - the heresy
known as" the divine right of kings." Basically, this is the old pagan
caesarism which placed the monarch above national law, instead of
under it as in Catholic kingdoms. The power and authority which
democracy arrogates to itself are not only absolute, but limitless. No
Caesar, no oriental despot ever possessed the unbridled political
potential latent in modern democracy.

The tyrannical "divine right of kings" which destroyed
Christendom has now become the divine right of the people. The
worst Christian monarchs never concentrated in their persons such
powers as are now wielded by the faceless kings of democracy. By
usurpation of the three powers of royalty without reference to God,
they not only make their own laws, but they implement and
interpret them at will. Democracy provides its own magisterium,
determining for itself the justice of its rule without reference to any
exterior moral authority. Such a hydra-headed monarchy dares to
rule minds as it does bodies.

THE UTOPIAN MAGISTERIUM

Article VI of the U.S. Constitution states in the second of its three provisions: "This Constitution, and the laws of the United States which shall be made in pursuance thereof; and all treaties made, or which shall be made, under the authority of the United States, shall be the supreme law of the land; and the judges in every State shall be bound thereby, anything in the Constitution or laws of any State to the contrary notwithstanding."

As often pointed out, the name of God is nowhere mentioned in this august document. Those "sovereign" States which ratified it were thereafter United in formally declaring themselves free of the fetters of Christendom. That an American Catholic can read such a statement without being struck with fear and consternation is incontrovertible proof that he is not so much a child of God as a child of the Revolution, born and bred in its ideology. Not only is he oblivious to blasphemy, he is insanely unconcerned about the punishments which must follow, and have followed, on public sins against justice. He accepts as normal that in politics, the Rights of Man are by some strange necessity, if not superior to the Rights of God, at least independent of them.

For him the Declaration of Independence which preceded the Constitution was little more than righteous defiance of a tyrannical monarch on the other side of the Atlantic who was asking for a come-uppance, as his history books assure him. He cannot see it for what it really was: the formal exclusion of God from the direction of public affairs. His blindness is not inculpable, but it is understandable. This Declaration, which the above Article VI encoded in 1787, two years before the French Revolution, was the prototype of those which would be adopted by nearly every nation in the world. Nothing like it has been seen since the revolt of Lucifer and his angels.

This has not always been the case. For instance, in 1837 a decree by King Charles Albert of Piedmont read:

The Apostolic Roman Catholic religion is the only religion of the State. The King is honored to be the protector of the Church and to promote the observance of its laws in matters of her competence. The highest State officials will watch diligently to maintain perfect harmony between Church and State ... Other religions already existing within the State are merely tolerated.

What King Charles Albert was voicing was not exceptional at the time and attracted little attention. For some 1500 years, following the lead of Clovis, King of the Franks, such was the accepted norm of government among Christians.

Unfortunately, the King of Piedmont's promulgation proved to be one of the last official testimonials to Christ's supreme sovereignty uttered by a Christian people. Already Christendom was gasping for breath on the eve of the revolutionary paroxysms which would devitalize Europe by the end of the century. Following the democratic "unification" of Italy, even the Papacy would be divested of the remaining temporal possessions which afforded it the modicum of financial independence indispensable to its spiritual role in the world. Since then we have seen the lamentable consequences of Rome's dependence on "Peter's Pence," which for a century has been wielded so effectively against her by a wealthy Americanist hierarchy and others of like mind.

For a time men acknowledged, as many still do, that authority was conferred by God and superseded all man-made legislation. Not only did the Magisterium of the Church not conflict in any way with the moral substructure of the surviving judicial systems, it was tacitly recognized as one of its main supports. Slowly but surely, however, as the Faith declined, the Christian form of government began to be viewed as an anachronism, an outgrown stage of political development useful in its day, but no longer suited to a better informed, more mature citizenry.

Because by its very nature self-government could not continue to recognize any moral force exerted upon itself from the outside, this had to be openly declared, at least in principle. In other words, some means of arbitrating the conflicts of interests which are a normal part of society had to be found without recourse or deference to the Holy Roman Catholic Church or any other holdover from the dark ages. Such conflicts must now be resolved, not according to antiquated Christian principles, but in the light of mankind's higher social concepts: liberty, equality and brotherhood. Or, as the American Declaration put it, "life, liberty, and the pursuit of happiness."

To this end, obviously the new utopia would have to have a Magisterium of its own to determine right and wrong in disputed cases. So the framers of the U.S. Constitution duly created one. Preceding Article VI which decrees the supremacy of their hand work, is Article III, which reads, "The judicial power of the United States shall be vested in one Supreme Court, and in such inferior courts as Congress may from time to time ordain and establish." Judges are appointed for life, assuming proper behavior, and their salaries may not be diminished. Section 2 states, "The judicial power shall extend to all cases, in law and equity, arising under this Constitution, etc." having in some cases original jurisdiction and in others appellate.

Following immediately on its declaration of constitutional supremacy, Article VI had laid down that members of this judiciary, like the executive and legislative branches of the new utopian state, "shall be bound by oath or affirmation, to support this Constitution; but no religious test shall ever be required as a qualification to any office or public trust under the United States." One must indeed be a child of the Revolution not to be unnerved by these words, which to a Christian constitute a hopeless contradiction. In the absence of any religious norm or authority, to whom, and by witness of whom, is oath or affirmation made? Our latter day innocent can only conclude that the modern democratic state, like God whom it presumes to displace, swears only by itself (*Jer. 22:5*).

If this be so, then it follows inevitably that the Constitution determines national morality, and indeed the task of defining it in any given case does ultimately fall to its created magisterium, the Supreme Court. Chief Justice Charles Evans Hughes put the matter very simply when he said, "The Constitution means what the Supreme Court says it means," - with all that follows therefrom. And a great deal does.

+

The trinitarian structure of the three branches of government under this supreme Constitution may not be merely coincidental. As we have seen, the interdependent (and presumably co-equal and co-existent) executive, legislative and judiciary parts of its mechanism are the three prerogatives of royalty. They are more than slightly reminiscent of the Persons of the Most Blessed Trinity. Whether the Founding Fathers had such a parody in mind, or whether the structure took shape as an inescapable consequence of created reality - which projects the divine image whether it will or no - is not within our competence to judge. We can only note that in their comportment both *intra* and *extra*, interiorly among themselves and exteriorly to the world at large, the three branches of the Constitution project a most disturbing analogy with the appropriated functions of the divine Persons.

Where the Executive can be seen to play the role of "Father," and the legislative that of the "Son," the Supreme Court seems to play the part of the Holy Ghost. As perfecter and interpreter, it has proved itself a dependable prophet of "the things that are to come," such as we could never have endured to hear straight off at the beginning of the *Novus Ordo Seclorum*. Since the founding of the United States this democratic paraclete has certainly had many things to say to us, "not speaking of itself, but what things soever it shall hear" that we never heard before (*John 16:12-13*). Whatever the source of its inspiration, the Court, like the Constitution, is Supreme throughout the land.

The parody becomes even more profane. Surprisingly enough, the Supreme Court has turned out to be the chosen instrument of the anti-Christ forces in the nation. In the early days of the United States the judicial arm was regarded as the weakest of the three branches of government, for it had no control over finances or the military. Much less could it make laws or implement them. In the continued exercise of its duties, however, the Court underwent an extraordinary metamorphosis: In some kind of pentecostal outburst, "It has developed ... to a position of equality in the governmental trinity, and in the minds of many it stands today as the most powerful of the traditional branches of government, especially through its function of declaring void the acts of Congress or of the executive when they are in conflict with the Constitution." In this "the federal judiciary is unique among the court systems of the world" and in fact" the balance wheel of the entire governmental system."

The roots of its unprecedented power are not hard to trace, for the Court's orientation was set very early. It was in the classical *Marbury v. Madison* decision, handed down in 1803, that Chief

Justice John Marshall established its right to declare the nullity of congressional acts. This right was in no way defined in the Constitution, but Justice Marshall set the federal precedent by following the lead of some state courts who before the adoption of the Constitution had on occasion declared statutes unlawful because of conflict with existing state laws.

> *Marshall's argument may be summarized as follows: (1) The Constitution is a superior law. (2) A legislative act contrary to the Constitution is therefore not a law. (3) It is always the duty of the court to decide between two conflicting laws. (4) If a legislative act conflicts with the superior law - the Constitution - it is clearly the duty of the court to refuse to apply the legislative act. (5) If the court does not refuse to apply such legislation, the foundation of all written constitutions is destroyed.*
>
> *This transcendent power has not gone undisputed. It has been pointed out that the Court is limited by the Constitution as well as the other two branches of government. By exercising final judicial review of the acts of the others, it may be exceeding its proper powers. In theory at least, the equality of the three departments is destroyed. If the Supreme Court has the power to void an act of Congress, and Congress has no immediate recourse, there can be little doubt that the court is the superior unit.*

The authority quoted here is *Government of the American People*, by Young, Manning and Arnold.

Congress does have one desperate recourse, however, and that is an amendment to the Constitution. Unpopular decisions led to the Eleventh and Sixteenth Amendments; the Dred Scott decision led to the Fourteenth Amendment. The strategy is cumbersome, but clear. Without debating the ramifications of this possibility, the position of the Supreme Court as ordinary moral arbiter of the acts of the United States must be conceded. Morality is what law is all about. If the Supreme Court were a Catholic body under a Constitution recognizing the Kingship of Christ as did that of King Charles Albert, the U.S. citizen would be enjoying the blessings of Christendom.

As we know, such is far from the case. We have a new, legally imposed morality which could only have been inspired by the father of lies himself. In principle natural law, divine law, ecclesiastical law, or in fact any law, is now subject to the "supreme" law of the Constitution, whose only moral arbiter is its own Supreme Court. Under such a dispensation, even the Ten Commandments can be repealed, and degrading vices declared legal. As the logical aftermath of widespread divorce and contraception, in 1973 even abortion became licit. Abortion is, after all, merely the extreme form of contraception.

That most heinous of crimes against the utterly defenseless has not only become commonplace, but is seen as a positive duty to society in certain cases. Even Catholics in public office with personal convictions to the contrary consider themselves bound by the Constitution to uphold this legal right to kill. Either they never heard or have chosen to forget Leo XIII's warning in *Immortale Dei* to the effect that "it is unlawful to follow one line of conduct in private life and another in public, respecting privately the authority of the Church, but publicly rejecting it."

In the name of protecting the rights of the mother, the American Magisterium has in effect decreed that because this kind of killing is not murder, the mother's right to do so must not be interfered with in any way. Her Court-given right to kill her infant even supersedes that infant's right to "life, liberty and the pursuit of happiness" guaranteed under the Constitution! There are therefore no penalties under the law for committing - within some prescribed limitations - an act once universally recognized as a particularly vicious infringement of the Fifth Commandment. At the same time, by the insane logic of utopia, outraged citizens who persist in defending the unborn's right to life guaranteed by almighty God can expect to be prosecuted mercilessly. Given the missionary zeal of some pro-abortionist jurists, their penalties have often proved excessive. John W. Whitehead, President of the Rutherford Institute, writing in the October 1990 issue of Action, had this to report:

> *A federal district court decision in New York presents a typical scenario. There the rescuers were charged with violating a federal law that prohibits the conspiracy to interfere with the civil rights of any protected group. The 'protected' group in this instance was pregnant women and the civil right*

was that of interstate travel. The federal judge there fined Operation Rescue more than $400,000. When asked why the fines were so high, the judge stated: 'I know these are high fines, but earlier fines were ignored and did not stop the protests ...(It) was necessary to take coercive action.' Therefore, the purpose of the heavy fines was not to punish the offense committed but to discourage future protests.

To keep a healthy grip on sanity, it helps to remember that Utopia owes its origin to a murder committed at the very dawn of history. Abortion is only one of its more sensational evils. The power of its Supreme Magisterium has been used even to outlaw prayer from the schools it supports, not neglecting at the same time to forbid the allocation of public funds to other schools where prayer might find a place. Much could be said regarding the Court's responsibility for the proliferation of other perversions, such as buggery, pornography, atheism, *in vitro* fertilization, surrogate motherhood or the systematic debauchery of children through sex education.

Legalized adultery masquerading as re-marriage has been long accepted as a way of life in the American Utopia, which was leading the world in divorce by the end of the 19th century. In practice this means polygamy and polyandry are also permitted, for as long as husbands and wives are enjoyed sequentially, one at a time, utopians may have as many as they please. The next step is clear. In the Washington Post for October 26, 1990 Ruth Marcus reported, "Retired Supreme Court Justice Lewis F. Powell Jr. told a group of law students that he regrets his 1986 vote upholding a Georgia statute that made homosexual sodomy a criminal offense." Aberrations which in countries once Christian incurred penalties under the law, are now protected by this same law, in the of name of freedom.

Aptly did Leo XIII declare in *Libertas Praestantissimum*, "To reject the supreme authority of God and to cast off all obedience to Him in public matters ... is the greatest perversion of liberty."

THE AMERICAN WAY

News photos of the uprising in Beijing in 1989 would indicate that America's talent for animating the common man to self-assertion has lost none of its power over two centuries. Apparently we are now a source of inspiration to the mysterious East as well as to the practical West. It was not Kwan-Ying, the Chinese goddess of mercy, who was set up as icon in Tianenmen Square, but a paper-maché Statue of Liberty, the Masonic Madonna of the United States. She was furthermore surrounded by banners and placards sporting the most hallowed American slogans (in English yet!) running all the way from "You can't cheat all of the people all of the time" to "Give me liberty or give me death!"

Sadly, the latter choice became all too real in the ensuing executions of some enthusiastic partisans. So what's new? As the illuminatus Thomas Jefferson said in his letter to Col. William S. Smith, "What signify a few lives lost in a century or two? ... The tree of liberty must be refreshed from time to time with the blood of patriots and tyrants. It is their natural manure." When his turn came to lead a revolution, Mao Zedong wouldn't put it any better in the saying attributed to him: "Even if 300,000,000 Chinese were killed in an atomic war, there would still be 300,000,000 left." Thus the revolutionary versions of Tertullian's famous, "Blood of martyrs is the seed of Christians."

Although brutally suppressed for the nonce, the situation in China, orchestrated in conjunction with the Baltic insurgence, German re-unification, Polish elections and upheavals at the very door of the Kremlin, gives every indication of being ordered to the final global realization of the old *Novus Ordo Seclorum* which has figured for over a half century on the American dollar bill. A political system whose justice resides not in moral law, but in equality, and whose liberty is produced by "rights" and not by the truth which makes men free, has nothing whatever in common with Christianity. That the widespread latter day conversion to warmed over democracy is in no way synonymous with the conversion promised unconditionally by our Lady at Fatima should in due time become painfully clear.

Rehearsed in the universities, the abortive Chinese revolt is easily traced to the 40,000 Chinese studying on American campuses. In the Washington Post for March 25,1989 Jay Matthews reported, "Many student protesters, asked about American influence, placed great emphasis on the power of the U.S. trade and technology to keep the Chinese government from violently suppressing the Tianenmen encampment. 'China has borrowed money from the USA,' said Victor Han, a student activist dressed in jeans, beige shirt and headband, declaring that he is 'unafraid of death.' 'If China doesn't solve the problem of students, the USA will put on pressure,' Han said." The U.S. did not stop the suppression, but that does not mean that pressures are not being applied. For many years' now American capital has been quietly making its way behind the Iron Curtain via international cartels peddling everything from luxury hotels to hamburgers.

That is the American Way. Back in 1776 the American Revolution proved an inspiration to every revolutionary in Europe, providing them with incontrovertible proof that a man-made secular state could be achieved by violent rupture with constituted authority. Before long a succession of similar eruptions broke out in both hemispheres of Christendom, toppling thrones and altars, separating states from Church and generally putting on top whatever was on the bottom.

The impetus to world revolution given by the American success became obscured as the United States settled down and became respectable, taking its place unobtrusively among the world powers, but in the 18th century its role was clearly recognized. One year before the outbreak of the French Revolution, the Marquis de Condorcet, one of its foremost architects and later one of its victims, actually wrote a propaganda piece entitled *The Influence of the American Revolution on Europe*. So closely was Europe watching developments on our shores, he had the year before composed "Letters from a New Hampshire Bourgeois to a Citizen of Virginia on the Uselessness of Dividing the Legislative Powers among Various Bodies." Then followed "Letters from a United States Citizen to a Frenchman on Current Matters."

The revolutionary intelligentsia in every nation on the Continent had been vitally interested in the American experiment from the beginning. How else explain the many foreigners who suddenly appeared out of nowhere to help the American cause, even occupying posts of command in the revolutionary militia? Is it coincidence that nearly all were Masons? Count Pulaski's battle flag sported the All-Seeing Eye and Triangle of the craft, with the words *Non Alius Regit*. As soon became plain, the American experiment had always been a global project.

Back in 1634 Our Lady had appeared in Quito, Ecuador to warn the faithful of what lay ahead for them. On February 2, feast of the Purification, announcing herself under the title "Our Lady of Good Fortune," she told Mother Mary Anne of Jesus Torres, "At the end of the 19th century and for a large part of the 20th, various heresies will flourish on this earth, which will have become a free republic." This Marian prophecy has been amply fulfilled.

By 1792, two years before his death in prison, Condorcet was peddling revolutionary ideology to Spain and Spanish America with spectacular results. In a preface to a 1945 edition of Condorcet's Opuscula, still largely unknown in the U.S., the Argentinean Alberto Palcos writes:

> *Indeed the U.S. is forging ahead in inaugurating a new stage in the history of humanity. Favored with two centuries of colonial life during which they enjoyed the liberties received from England, they adopt a wise republican system of government and proclaim the new rights ... The United States are providing the world a lesson.*

Condorcet's little work, says he, is "irrefutable evidence today of the importance the apostles of liberty on the old continent attached to the North American show, and its projection on the French Revolution.

> *Condorcet presents it both as an example and a warning to Europe. He points out the colossal advantages gained by a nation which eliminates odious and unjust differences from its bosom, diffuses education and promotes wellbeing. Inevitably it will attract caravans of immigrants and will stimulate agriculture, industry and international trade; it desires this without let, freely, without limit. A country under such conditions is like a benediction. It is destined to transform itself into a powerful agent of world peace, etc., etc.*

By the mid-nineteenth century, America was inspiring Germany with these hopes. The well-known painting of George Washington standing perilously upright in an open boat crossing the Delaware was not painted in the United States. Nor could it have been contemporary, for the large flapping Stars and Stripes behind him had not been officially adopted. The scene was a studio piece done in Germany in 1850 by Emanuel Leutze, who hoped thereby to rekindle among his discouraged compatriots the fires of the failed German revolution of 1848. When last heard of, the original painting was stored in the basement of the Metropolitan Museum, "neither history nor art," in the opinion of its President, William S. Collin. Its place in American iconography is secure, however, for reproductions abound and its propaganda value remains undiminished.

Leo XIII, a liberal Pope who conceded whatever was possible to modern democracy, nevertheless minced no words in *Immortale Dei*: "Inciting to revolution is treason, not only against man, but against God." Because all authority is ultimately derived from God, it may not be unseated at will once it is established. Revolution is not restoration. It is what the word says it is: an overturning. Revolution is disobedience, a major sin against the Fourth Commandment which draws whole populations behind it.

Most Catholics who have grown up in its shadow here in the United States have absorbed its ideology with their mothers' milk and will therefore admit only with great difficulty that revolution *per se* is a bad thing. For them it is a cherished tradition, one peculiarly their own, and a benefit to be shared with others. Besides, they will tell you, their revolution was not like others. It was different. The fact remains that it was the first of a whole string of modern revolts against the royal Kingship of Christ, and serious historians are now beginning to explore their interlocking leadership.

In the Anatomy of Revolution, Crane Brinton scrutinizes some of the similarities in the English, American, French and Russian revolutions. He points out that all without exception were "from the left." Democracy, as Lenin had been quick to point out in *State and Revolution*, "is only one of the stages in the course of developments from feudalism to capitalism and from capitalism to communism." In each case, notes Brinton, "the existing government attempted to collect monies from people who refused to pay." That these people were not unable to pay, but refused to do so makes for an important distinction.

> *These were all societies on the whole on the upgrade before the revolution carne, and the revolutionary movements seem to originate in the discontents of not unprosperous people who feel restraint, cramp, annoyance, rather than downright crushing oppression. Certainly these revolutions are not started by down-and-outers, by starving, miserable people. These revolutionists are not worms turning, not children of despair. These revolutions are born of hope, and their philosophies are formally optimistic ... Untouchables very rarely revolt.*

In other words, revolutionaries tend to be those "who find an intolerable gap between what they have come to want - their' needs' - and what they actually get." A Catholic has no difficulty recognizing this as simple covetousness, one of the seven deadly sins.

For Brinton, the typical revolutionary is Figaro, anti-hero of the Beaumarchais plays and the Rossini opera. A truly luciferian personage, Figaro is the barber of a wealthy lord to whom he considers himself intrinsically superior in every way. He is convinced that were it not for an accident of birth and the injustice of prevailing institutions, his innate intelligence and *savoir-faire* would guarantee him a rank at least equal to his master's. He finds sufficient proof in the way his master utterly depends on him. Personified in Figaro is the democratic dogma that all men are created equal, the I'm-as-good-as-the-next-man syndrome. Given the opportunity, "I can be anything I want to be." God's will does not figure.

A little violence is deemed a small price to pay to open up the proper opportunities to the Figaros of this world. Yet, as Brinton points out, revolutions in their first stages are characterized by dramatic rather than really serious bloodshed. "The hated old regime has been conquered so easily: The way is open to the regeneration men have been so long talking about, hoping for ..." What follows is of course quite different. It will be objected that our American Revolution was at no time guilty of the excesses of the French or the Russian. This may be, but in its own American way it exhibited many terrorist aspects which go unmentioned by the victors who write the history texts.

Portrayed as a conflict between homespun native Americans pitted against tyrannical, greedy foreigners, our Revolution was in fact like all others, a civil war between blood brothers. Quite understandably, England has never viewed it as anything else. During the War of 1812 the Times noted:

> *There is no public feeling in this country stronger than indignation against the Americans. That [they] should have attempted to plunge the parricidal weapon into the heart of that country from which its own origin was derived ... this is conduct so black, so loathesome, so hateful, that it naturally stirs up the indignation we have described.*

Many colonials agreed at the time, for statistically almost as many fought for England as against her. Reprisals against those remaining faithful to their King were cruel, effective, relentless and largely economic. Properties worth millions were summarily confiscated without compensation. The Simsbury copper mines earned the title "Newgate of Connecticut" after they were transformed into dungeons for Loyalist prisoners. One distinguished inmate was Benjamin Franklin's only son William, Governor of New Jersey under the British, and a staunch Tory.

At the grass roots were tarring and feathering.

> *On August 8, 1775, riflemen took a man in New Milford, Connecticut, a most incorrigible Tory, who called them d-d rebels ... and made him walk before them to Litchfield, which is twenty miles, and carry one of his own geese in his hand. When they arrived there they tarred and feathered him and made him pluck his goose, and then bestowed the feathers on him, drummed him out of the company and obliged him to kneel down and thank them for their lenity.*

For more on this subject, the reader is referred to Crane Brinton or to Wallace Brown's "The Loyalists and the American Revolution" in *Myth and the American Experience.*

Unlike their European counterparts, Americans had the advantage of being able to expropriate an area geographically removed from their motherland. In their New Atlantis they could repudiate their origins physically as well as morally. As citizens of a nation of their own fabrication, they could assume with relative ease whatever identities they deemed fit. As in that first artificial city which Cain named after his son, everything in the American Utopia would be young and new. An interesting facet of the revolt unearthed by sociologists is that it spawned quite spontaneously a whole vocabulary of contempt for the elderly. Words like *geezer, baldy, oldster, old goat* suddenly entered the vocabulary for the first time; whereas *grandame, gramfer, granther, granam, beldam, grandsire* and other common terms of respect for the aged began unaccountably to disappear, and are now gone for good.

Utopia does not look kindly on citizens considered not only "unproductive," but who might be old enough to remember saner times and tell the children about them. Where only youth is worthy of reverence, we may suspect that He whom Scripture characterizes as "the Ancient of Days" is the true target, and not mere injustice and oppression. Like Cain, revolutionaries can bear neither the past nor the present. The former must be forgotten and the latter perpetually anticipated. Everything must be planned. Like all utopians, revolutionaries can live only in the future, because the future has no real existence.

That the American rebel leaders were not highly esteemed by the generality leaps out from contemporary documents. Franklin and Jefferson were regarded with well-founded suspicion. When Jefferson sold Congress his library for $23,950 in 1814, public indignation dubbed the collection "atheistical, irreligious and immoral." As for George Washington, Franklin's grandson probably voiced the most extreme opinion in the Philadelphia Aurora: "If ever a nation was debauched by a man, the American nation has been by Washington." Strong words, but the first President was remembered, among other things, as a wealthy real estate entrepreneur who had not scrupled to stake out for himself land to the west which was off limits to others.

It was not until the 20th century and the sculptures on Mount Rushmore that Washington and Jefferson really joined the demigods. By that time the myth had been implanted in the popular mind that the U.S. was founded as a Christian nation on Christian principles, just because it was preponderately populated by Christians. The Founding Fathers, who seldom if ever referred to the Deity in any but the vaguest, most impersonal Masonic terms, are now regarded as devout believers. Historical fact and Washington's own testimony say otherwise. Even those who did believe in the Christian God had no use for Catholics. One was John Adams, who made fun of their worship in his private letters and coined the phrase, "Catholic Christians, cabalistic Christians."

In the days when our one-ounce postage was thirteen cents (a sacred number in Masonry) a Christmas stamp featured Washington praying on his knees at Valley Forge. There had been a similar one in 1928, a bronze version of which was set into the Sub-Treasury Building in New York. To date the Parson Weems who was responsible for the cherry tree story remains the sole authority for his alleged piety. More in character is the stained glass window in the Prayer Room set up in the Senate in 1954, where Washington is shown deep in prayer before the Great Seal of the United States.

The truth is that Washington, like Jefferson and others, was known to attend church services only rarely and for official reasons. Rupert Hughes, a well-known debunker of the 30's, tells us Washington had long ceased attending his own church after the pastor rebuked him for never receiving communion, a practice Washington disagreed with on principle. In 1776 the Continental Congress actually decreed a day of prayer and fasting "to confess and bewail our manifold sins ... through the merits and mediation of Jesus Christ," which proves that there were indeed Christians in that body. When Washington passed the order on to his men, however, he deleted the reference to our Lord.

On his deathbed he was not heard to mention God or religion, and in his will he left no bequests to any religious cause. Despite all evidence to the contrary, however, American Catholics will relate the story of his "vision of Our Lady" at Valley Forge and his last minute conversion to the Faith. The latter has been conveyed through the years by Americanist historians without a shred of documentation beyond a rumor that Fr. Francis Neale, S.J., of Georgetown had been summoned to Mount Vernon and spent four hours with Washington some time before he died. If the visit occurred, for all posterity knows its purpose may have been to discuss the transfer of some real estate. But doubtless such fictions proved useful in steering reluctant Catholics into the proper American Way.

By now the American Catholic Church is:

> *... no more than a miserable affluent of the great movement of apostasy being organized in every country for the establishment of a One World Church which shall have neither dogmas, nor hierarchy, neither discipline for the mind, nor curb for the passions, and which, under the pretext of freedom and human dignity, would bring back to the world (if such a church could overcome) the reign of legalized cunning and force, and the oppression of the weak and of all those who toil and suffer.*

These words, addressed to the French democrats of the Sillon in 1910, sadly apply to the body of the faithful in the U.S. today.

There had been such an outcry against Masonry in the early 19th century, that an American anti-Masonic political party actually took shape, formed by those who recognized the anti-Christian character of Masonic naturalism and the power it wielded in their national government. Strangely enough, pamphlets of the period exposing Masonry seem to have been penned exclusively by Protestants and Protestant divines. Despite the many papal condemnations of the Craft, none of the polemic was carried on by Catholics. In the wake of the Know-Nothings and the convent burnings, these evidently preferred to keep a low profile in the new pluralistic society where freedom ruled, rather than risk the consequences of speaking out against the occult power. For over a century now, God the Founding Father personified by Washington, seated in glory amid the rosy clouds inside the Capitol dome, has gone unchallenged.

"We fear that worse is yet to corne," wrote St. Pius X. "The end result of this developing promiscuousness, the beneficiary of this cosmopolitan social action, can only be a democracy which will be neither Catholic, nor Protestant nor Jewish. It will be a religion more universal than the Catholic Church, uniting all men become brothers and comrades at last." In the U.S. this kind of religion, based on an accepted political mythology, has been flourishing too long to cause comment.

Whither the American Way? To obey constituted authority is a Christian precept, "For there is no power but from God, and those that are, are ordained of God. Therefore he that resisteth the power, resisteth the ordinance of God. And they that resist, purchase to themselves damnation" (*Rom. 13:1-2*). We may assume from these words of St. Paul that he disapproved of flag burning, but he also disapproved of passing off false doctrine as true. Early Christians were martyred for refusing to burn incense to the Emperor. Must they now burn incense to the People?

"Catholic doctrine tells us," says St. Pius X, "that the primary duty of charity does not lie in the toleration of false ideas, however sincere they may be, nor in the theoretical or practical indifference towards the errors and vices in which we see our brethren plunged, but in the zeal for their intellectual and moral improvement as well as for their material wellbeing."

Unlike the Revolution, the Church:

> *... does not have to free herself from the past ... All that is needed is to take up again, with the help of the true workers for a social restoration, the organizations which the Revolution shattered, and to adapt them, in the same Christian spirit which inspired them, to the new environment arising from the material developments of today's society. Indeed, the true friends of the people are neither revolutionaries nor innovators, they are traditionalists.*

Theirs is not the American Way. They would rather try to follow the One who told them, "I am the Way."

THE USAN CATHOLIC

In these latter days humanity has been confronted with a choice between two political systems which are irreconcilable: the sovereignty of the people, or the sovereignty of God. Obviously, both can't be sovereign.

The first system is concerned exclusively with man's temporal needs and aspirations, his "life, liberty and the pursuit of happiness" on earth, ends good in themselves, as far as they go. Government is non-hierarchical and democratic, based on a rationally constructed order. Authority rises upward from the people, in whom sovereignty resides.

National unity lies in the equality or "brotherhood" of its citizens under the law. Its buzzwords are liberty and justice for all. Taking no cognizance of original sin, this type of government assumes that human nature will automatically reach truth and do the right thing if it is left sufficiently free to do so. Religion is politically irrelevant, or at best a private matter. The Kingship of Jesus Christ, although not formally denied, has no foothold.

The second system is also concerned with man's temporal needs, but *sub specie aeternitatis*, with a view to his supernatural eternal destiny. Government is hierarchical and non-democratic, based on family and the natural order, which presumes inequality. Authority descends from God and resides in leaders who tend by the very nature of God's order to be hereditary. National unity resides in the person of its king, much as the unity of the Church resides in the Vicar of Christ. Its watchwords are obedience and love.

Given man's fallen nature, this type of government recognizes that without monitoring, freedom of speech automatically leads to error, and freedom of action to evil. It formally acknowledges the Kingship of the Son of God to whom "all power" - not just spiritual power - "has been given" (*Matt. 28:18*). This is the view taken by that "eldest son of the Church," King Clovis of the Franks. Formally adopted by every European nation one after the other it reduced the miracle we call Christendom. It was the political norm of the west for a millennium and a half until the late 18th century, when the democratic system gained ascendancy and gradually obliterated the Catholic state. Today only a few small governments like Colombia, Liechtenstein, the Dominican Republic or Monaco still acknowledge Christ's Kingship by statute.

The United States has never at any time been one of these. As we have seen, it was the first nation on earth to be "conceived in liberty," founded from its inception on the Rights of Man without reference to any outside authority, human or divine. The name of God is eloquently absent from its Constitution. A more perfect mirror image of the nation founded by Clovis could scarcely be found than the United States. Christ the King, Lord of heaven and earth, is not only ignored on principle, but is replaced by a sovereign ruler known as "We the people" whose general will, to use Rousseau's terminology, is law. Under a Constitution making no provision for any moral standard outside itself, the people are the only source of its morality. With so treacherous a foundation to sustain it, public morality never rises above that prevailing in the majority.

Hell justly appreciates the power of the people. Fr. Theodore Geiger of Bamberg Cathedral tells of an exorcism in the last century which uncovered a posse of demons led by one calling himself "Caesar," whose specialty was setting governments against the Church. They told the exorcist, "The world wants to be on our side. Our most reliable shock troops are the people!" After all, wasn't it the people who were manipulated into demanding our Lord's Crucifixion? Why not depend on them to do the same for His Church?

One would normally expect open warfare between Catholics and utopian democrats, two parties whose views of political reality are so radically different. And indeed such bade fair to be the case early on in the New Atlantis, especially in Puritan New England in the days of the American Protective Association and the Know-Nothings. Convents were burned, and Catholics were openly discriminated against. These anti-Catholics saw quite clearly the incompatibility of the two political systems, even if many Catholics did not. Like de Tocqueville, the convent-burners knew perfectly well that Catholicism is "the natural enemy of democracy."

But everything settled down in due time with the steady growth of Americanism, that handy heresy which specifically holds that the two views of political reality are actually perfectly compatible, and their differences only apparent. Its promoters believed that with proper inculturation, Catholics could subscribe at the same time to the Faith of the Apostles and the ideals of the Revolution. Needless to say, those who espoused this devastating error labored to prove themselves as red, white and blue as the next man, and they began exhibiting a coloration all their own.

Appropriating a useful word recently coined in Europe for anything pertaining to the United States, we shall call them "Usan" Catholics rather than American Catholics, because their lineage is not derived from the Catholic America whose culture flourished for three centuries after Columbus. Usan Catholicism owes its identity entirely to the United States, having germinated in the 13 colonies of those lately arrived English heretics who managed to wedge themselves permanently between the territories of Spain and France, the two great Catholic powers who once controlled the continent. Proclaiming their independence of everybody in 1776, these colonists then proceeded, as we have seen, to set themselves up as a *Novus Ordo Seclorum* - bad Latin for "New Deal" - which would provide the future pattern for the union not only of states, but of entire nations, without ecclesiastical interference of any kind.

In due time, as the Spirit of '76 progressively infiltrated their religious life, the Catholic components of the new regime became less and less distinguishable from the generality of the population - and more and more distinguishable from the rest of the Holy Catholic Church. In 1899 Pope Leo XIII was constrained to write the Apostolic Letter *Testem Benevolentiae* to call attention to their singularity, which he dubbed Americanism. He warned them that the Church in America must not try to be "different from what it is in the rest of the world."

To all practical purposes his Letter fell on deaf ears. Cardinal Gibbons, the Primate to whom it was addressed, made it public only after the secular press began printing excerpts from it culled from *L'Osservatore Romano*. The heresy had become so integral a part of the ecclesiastical power structure that, if it hadn't been for anguished protests to Rome on the part of a few courageous bishops and the Germans of the Midwest, Usan Catholics might never have become aware of how different they really were, but they would end by taking pride in it. In the spring of 1989, at the meeting of the American Bishops, Cardinal May would tell John Paul II, "Things are different in America. We have liberty and freedom, we don't look at the Pope as having total jurisdiction. We are different!"

Where did this Americanism corne from? Certainly not from the Protestants, much less from Masons or atheists intent on forcing hapless Catholics to a new way of thinking against their better judgment. Not even Francis Bacon could be blamed for it. No outside force would have been equal to the task. From the beginning Americanism was a specifically Catholic heresy. An early form of Modernism, it was originally an Anglo-Irish importation which antedated the United States and grew up with it, having arrived on these shores with the first boatloads of English Catholics who settled Lord Baltimore's Maryland colony in 1633.

Lord Baltimore had made a previous attempt at a spot called Avalon in Newfoundland, but it had failed, and actually there is reason to believe that even this was not the first English Catholic colony. The "Lost Colony" in Virginia, planted on Roanoke Island by Sir John Grenville in 1585, and which disappeared mysteriously without a trace, may have been composed of Catholics. If this is true, Virginia Dare, the first English child born in the New World, would have been a Catholic.

Although Baltimore and most of his colonists were supposedly Catholic, his own antecedents remain shrouded in mystery, and from the beginning the venture was an unabashed experiment in ecumenism, one in which diligent "merchants of light" must have had a hand. Dedicated to religious liberty and freedom of conscience, the colony included many Protestants and perhaps even some Jews posing as Protestants. This explains why all persuasions worshiped in the same church building, and why the Catholic Lord Proprietor directed "all Roman Catholiques to be silent upon all occasions of discourse concerning matters of religion." Needless to say, the Protestants soon took over, and the Catholics suffered the same persecution in Maryland as they had in England and the other English possessions.

The Masonic principle of religious plurality survived, however, and eventually found its way into the U.S. Constitution. Its main channel would be the Jesuit John Carroll, a Maryland descendant of Lord Baltimore's attorney general, and truly the Founding Father of Americanism. Educated abroad, he had been thoroughly converted to the political ideology of the Revolution by Gallican professors in the English expatriate colleges. After winning independence from England, the new government was unwilling to continue recognizing the jurisdiction of the Vicar Apostolic in London, so on the powerful recommendation of Benjamin Franklin, Carroll was appointed superior of the American missions.

The two men had become fast friends on a mission to Canada, on which they had been sent in an attempt to persuade that country to join the Revolution. The ruling establishment were desirous of a native prelate of their own political stripe who could be counted on to keep the Catholics in line, so when a Bishop was called for, Carroll once more proved to be the only acceptable candidate. Concerned for souls in so difficult a situation, Pope Pius VI erected the See of Baltimore and reluctantly approved their choice. Even so, Carroll would not take the oath until the Vatican omitted the obligation "to extirpate heretics."

This was 1789, a banner year for the forces of revolutionary democracy. It marked not only the installation of the first Usan Catholic Bishop in the world's first secular utopia, but the triumph of the French Revolution, the ratification of the U.S. Constitution, the inauguration of George Washington as first President of the new state, and the founding of Georgetown University. In the final analysis, the last event may have contributed most to the formation of the Usan Catholic, because the educational orientation of the Georgetown Jesuits influenced all the other Catholic institutions throughout the country. Eventually it would spawn not only the liberal Catholic University of America, but that "nursery of bishops", the North American College in Rome itself.

Because the Society of Jesus was under suppression at the time, Bishop Carroll and his brothers in religion acted as "the Incorporated Clergy of Maryland" to establish the College. In the statement of "Proposals" which they drew up to solicit support for their idea, the words "God" and "Catholic" are as conspicuous by their absence as they are in the U.S. Constitution. The college welcomed all faiths, although its primary goal was making good Americans of Catholics who would occupy influential positions in public life. Its first student was William Gaston, later an associate justice of the North Carolina supreme court. Visitors admiring the old murals on the walls of Georgetown's Gaston Hall will find little in them of Catholic inspiration.

The school's location had been selected long before by a mysterious Jesuit rumored to have been related to Queen Elizabeth. He was Fr. Thomas Copley, alias "Philip Fisher," who had also played a decisive role in the foundation of the ecumenical Maryland colony. His first choice for a site is now occupied by the U.S. Capitol, and the map of Washington, D.C. shows a clear geometric relationship between the two as points of a triangle with the Washington Monument in its center. The Seal of this Catholic university features an eagle with the blazon *E Pluribus Unum* in its beak, clutching a cross in one claw (the left one!) and a globe surmounted by a compass in the other, the whole surmounted by what appears to be an Irish harp! A variation of this crest is minus the compass and bears the devise *Utraque unum.*

This insignia is of a piece with the Usan ideography of Carroll's episcopal crest, which exemplifies perfectly the new American Church: Its central logo is a figure of the Blessed Virgin bearing the divine Infant, surrounded by a ring of stars. If the unwary Catholic didn't count them, he would assume that these are the twelve stars with which our Lady is crowned in the Apocalypse as personal symbol of the Church. Such is not the case, however, for there are thirteen stars, and therefore represent neither the apocalyptic luminaries, nor the traditional Apostles, nor the Twelve Tribes of Israel or anything the Catholic would expect. They can only represent the thirteen colonies of the new Masonic republic, presumably endorsed in this fashion by the Mother of God herself.

Artful duplicity worthy of a Cathar or an Albigensian! It is no surprise that Carroll's first cathedral was not of Gothic inspiration, but a classic temple in Enlightenment style designed by Benjamin Latrobe, Masonic architect of the Capitol. It is still one of the glories of Baltimore. In 1990 on the Feast of the Assumption, Archbishop William H. Keeler, then incumbent of the See of Baltimore, delivered the homily at a Mass at Lulworth Castle in England commemorating Carroll's consecration on that spot 200 years ago. The *Arlington Catholic Herald* quoted him as saying that John Carroll would be happy with the Church in the United States today. There is every reason to believe he would, for nearly every reform he had hoped for has now been adopted, not only in the United States, but in the Church worldwide: ecumenism, vernacularization, liturgical adaptation, collegiality and more.

+

Building on its auspicious beginnings, Americanism has dominated the Faith in the American Utopia without significant interruption until the present day. Maintaining a stranglehold on an unparalleled Catholic school system and ably aided by a liberal Catholic media, Americanist prelates like Cardinal Gibbons, Archbishop Ireland and Archbishop Keane were able to carry on the work begun by John Carroll and insure its spectacular fruition in the twentieth century. Urged as soon as they got off the boat to shed whatever cultural trappings they may have brought over with them, Catholic immigrants almost overnight were turned into fervent utopians, all the while continuing to frequent Mass and the Sacraments.

Where the first priority was to make Catholics good Americans, a most unbelievable and paradoxical result was achieved: The separation of Church and state, on which both Utopia and Americanism rest as upon dogmatic rock, proved to be the means of welding the two into one! To all practical purposes, the Usan Catholic has come to see absolutely no difference between the ideals of one and the other. In his eyes the Declaration of Independence and the Constitution have assumed the authority of Holy Writ. They are inerrant. If anything goes wrong politically, it is only because these sacred writings were not adhered to. On the occasion of Washington's Birthday, Cardinal Gibbons wrote in the Catholic Review that he was "ever more convinced that the Constitution of the United States is the greatest instrument of government that ever issued from the hand of man. That within the short space of one hundred years we have grown to be a great nation is due to the Constitution."

Under the circumstances, Catholic schools could hardly have been expected to single out for emphasis any Catholic doctrine which had the misfortune to conflict with the prevailing ideology, nor did they. In practice parochial administrators were fatally drawn to model their textbooks and their pedagogy as closely as possible on that of the public school system. Catechisms followed suit, not by teaching outright heresy, but by judiciously omitting or softening truths deemed politically incorrect in Utopia.

Nowhere in the Baltimore Catechisms is liberalism referred to as a sin. As for Gibbons' own catechism, *Faith of Our Fathers*, he is known to have openly boasted, "There is not one word in it that can give offense to our Protestant brethren." As a consequence, Catholic school children were taught to survive as Catholics in a pluralistic society, not by confrontation, much less by evangelization or any kind of witnessing, but by consistent accommodation to the environment. It was not charity, but "I getting along" which became the supreme virtue.

Because there is no place for the supernatural in Utopia, the inevitable happened. The very force of created reality drove American democracy to forge its own religion to fill the vacuum. Out of sheer desperation, the natural order rose above itself and attempted to fulfill the function of the divine. The result is an American variety of secular humanism which is the *de facto* state religion. After all, religion is what revolution is all about.

The net result is that the Catholic child in the U.S. grows up with two religions which get closer all the time. Alongside the Catholic liturgical year runs that of the secular government, where the Fourth of July seems to figure as a kind of Easter, Labor Day as Pentecost; Thanksgiving Day as the national Holy Thursday, Memorial Day as All Souls, and so on. And let's not forget Earth Day, Halloween and Secretaries Day, all part of the secular liturgical cycle, where Mother's Day does for the Assumption and Father's Day for a quasi-feast of St. Joseph. Happy Holidays!

There is also a sanctoral cycle, which Bishop Carroll may have initiated, for it was at his suggestion that February 22 was first set aside to honor George Washington. The Usan child is invited to venerate a whole bevy of such anti-heroes, most of whom were not even nominal Christians, let alone Catholics. To the revolutionaries - who would have been hanged for treason had they not won the war - have been added Abraham Lincoln, Rev. Martin Luther King and other secular saints soliciting our reverence. Even characters like John Brown, a psychopath with a weakness for ritual mutilations, find their way into the growing hagiography. The Nation's capital is studded with their shrines and holy places: the Lincoln Memorial, the Jefferson Memorial, the Washington Monument, the White House, almost all without exception dedicated by Masonic ceremonies.

The U.S. Capitol, filled with statuary, is a veritable St. Peter's - to which it has been compared by enthusiasts - where below stairs pilgrims may purchase national mementos, medals and devotional literature. The interior of the main cupola sets the tone, displaying the blasphemous "Apotheosis" of Washington reigning in heaven flanked by assorted deities, the work of *Constantino Brumidi*, a Mason who once restored frescoes at the Vatican. And of course, in the nearby Senate may be seen the Prayer Room with its stained glass window, flanked by two menorahs, on which Washington is shown kneeling under the Great Seal of the United States. To question any of this would be clearly "unpatriotic."

Like all religions, this secular faith has its hymns, its banners, its sacramentals, to support the national mythology. And of course there are idols to worship. Besides those at the national shrines, there is the great Masonic Madonna known as the Statue of Liberty, work of the Masonic engineer Gustave Eiffel and the Masonic sculptor Frederic Bartholdi. Dedicated with the customary Masonic ceremonies, the iron "Mother of Exiles," wielding her electric torch and sporting her spiked diadem, has greeted all arrivals in New York harbor since 1882. Recently she was invoked by student demonstrators in China.

+

But what harm is there in all this? No one takes official mythology all that seriously! One is reminded of the early Christians who were urged to satisfy the Roman authorities by offering a pinch of incense to the gods, "because nobody believes in them anyway." The harm is that by gradual inculturation, the ideals of utopia seep into the Faith. Although Rome never gave permission, for generations the Star-Spangled Banner had the distinction of being the only national flag in the world to be placed inside the Catholic sanctuary next to the Altar. Nowadays in some parish churches on the Fourth of July, the Pledge of Allegiance is offered to it. National anthems of Protestant or Masonic inspiration are sung at Mass without causing surprise. In the Byzantine Chapel in the National Shrine of the Immaculate Conception in Washington, D.C., the Statue of Liberty shares a mosaic with Our Lady of Perpetual Help.

Although the ideals of Utopia have long enjoyed quasi-canonization, until now they never intruded into the Catholic liturgy. But since Vatican II this is no longer the case. The Sacramentary approved by the Usan Catholic Bishops in 1985 actual contains a *Preface for Independence Day and Other Civic Observances* for use at the Holy Sacrifice of the Mass. Addressing God the Father and speaking of God the Son, this Preface reads in part, "His message took form in the vision of our fathers as they fashioned a nation where men might live as one. This message lives on in our midst as a task for men today and a promise for tomorrow." Such words come dangerously close to canonizing the U.S. Constitution by ascribing its authorship to Jesus Christ. One irreverent young wag has suggested that Roman candles be used on the altar for the Fourth of July, set to go off at the Consecration.

Still, this is only part of the harm. Inculturation of this kind not only introduces profane elements into the Faith, it cuts Catholics off from the mainstream of their true history and culture. By eliminating the supernatural dimension every child must have to reach his full moral stature, it dooms him to a deadly spiritual provincialism. Trapped in his immediate surroundings, his vision is shortened to the merely natural, the visible, accidental here and now. Heaven disappears from view, and hell is Halloween. The Catholic faith isn't tied to any culture, but every culture it touches is invested with new life. Without supplanting or disturbing any of their variety, it confers on all of them a profoundly Catholic resemblance. When the process is reversed, wine turns into water, theology degenerates into ideology, and truth tends to become whatever we read in the papers.

The inculturated Catholic has no past to sustain him. For him the Catholic history of this continent is irrelevant, because what little of it he is acquainted with occurred only after 1776, despite the fact that before the English settlements, colonial America was wholly Catholic and antedated the upstart republic by three centuries. How many schoolchildren have ever heard of Fr. Margil, Apostle of Texas? Or that Spanish Jesuits were martyred in Virginia, French Jesuits in New York? That Long Island was once called the Isle of the Apostles, and the Mississippi was the River of the Holy Spirit? Do they know that Our Lady of Guadalupe - and not the Statue of Liberty - is Patroness of the Americas? That the Cherokee alphabet was probably the work of a Belgian priest who was the great Chief Sequoia's uncle? And how about Venerable Mary of Agreda, who not only wrote our Lady's biography, but miraculously catechized the Indians of New Mexico?

The history which was not taught, even in Catholic schools, would fill textbooks to overflowing, for relegated to oblivion are no trifling minority, but the vast majority of the inhabitants of this hemisphere. What history is taught is highly selected, and until recently, tailored to WASP prejudices. The well-known Black

Legend has been used to maximum effect, conveying a Catholic past which bears little resemblance to reality. Students are led to believe that whatever misfortunes Catholic countries may have suffered were the consequence of their benighted religion, which even now prevents them from enjoying freedom in its fullness. In song and story Catholic sovereigns like Philip II are portrayed as sadists, and English pirates like Francis Drake as saviors. The heroes who suffered and died to bring the Faith and the benefits of Christendom to these shores go unmentioned. The denigrations of Columbus are too widespread to require mention.

Faith alone dissolves the deceits of Utopia, which might have been easily forestalled by judicious exposure in school to the political thought of Joseph de Maistre, Louis Veuillot, Soloviev or Donoso Cortes - if not to the headier ideas of Charles Maurras. Unfortunately, only English Catholic thinkers get much of a hearing, and more often than not they are liberals like Cardinal Newman or Lord Acton. Even Chesterton, alas, was partial to the French Revolution. With the incomparable school system at their disposal, one could expect that Usan Catholics would have become acquainted with at least the basics of St. Thomas, who taught clearly that the very notion of order chiefly consists in inequality, and that wherever the secular power erects obstacles to salvation, it must bow to the ecclesiastical.

Schools truly Catholic would have demonstrated that the principle of separation of Church and state is at best a legal fiction which can never work in practice; that Church and state, although distinct in their functions, must cooperate by the very fact that they rule the same human subject, namely, the citizen. The enormous political implications of devotion to the Sacred Heart would have been explained. By the same token, a huge deposit of papal teaching on the evils of democracy, much of which cannot even be found in English, might have been translated and disseminated according to the mind of the Church.

This teaching runs from Pius VI on down to Pius XII without interruption. It reached a climax with Pius IX's mighty *Syllabus of Errors*, a document which Archbishop Ireland of St. Paul feared "might be construed here as condemning our system of religious toleration" and might "furnish a pretext to the fanatics to persecute us." Condemned Propositions #55, 77, 78 and 79 of the *Syllabus* particularly alarmed him, and he insisted they simply didn't apply to America. The *Chicago Tribune* for January 19, 1865, however, voiced the plain truth, namely that the *Syllabus* was " directly in conflict with the Constitution of the U.S. and of every state in the Union." The same traditional teaching is found in Leo XIII's great social encyclicals, as well as in his Apostolic Letters *Longinqua Oceani* and *Testem Benevolentiae*, specifically addressed to American Catholics.

The most thunderous voice raised against the evils of democracy was of course that of Leo's successor St. Pius X, author of the encyclical on Modernism. In his Letter to the Sillon, exposing as it does the innate contradictions of so-called Christian Democracy, St. Pius makes his own the words of Leo XIII regarding "a certain Democracy which goes so far in its wickedness as to place sovereignty in the people and aims at the suppression of classes and their leveling down." For obvious reasons, this Letter has never been publicized in the U.S. and was not even translated until fairly recently. Outside traditionalist circles it is still virtually unknown.

Pius XI continued the losing battle, but it was too late. Finally, in 1925, in a last desperate effort, he established the feast of Christ the King, declaring from the Chair of Peter that nations as well as individuals owe public homage to Jesus Christ. Yet, two years later this same Pope condemned Charles Maurras' Action Francaise and soon after that disbanded the Cristeros in Mexico. Pope Pius XII lifted the ban on the Action Francaise immediately on his accession to the papal throne, and in 1955 was still pleading the Catholic position when he said in a discourse on September 7, "The Church does not conceal the fact that she considers collaboration between Church and State as normal and that she regards as ideal the unity of the people in the true religion and unanimity of action between her and the state."

Authoritative pronouncements such as these on the true nature of democracy have not been lacking, but have been imparted very sparingly to the faithful. Nor are they well received today by Catholics still believing it is America's "Manifest Destiny" to convert the world to the American Way. As Archbishop Ireland told the French in 1895:

Much as I believe that God governs men and nations, I believe that a divine mission has been assigned to the Republic

*of the United States. That mission is to prepare the world, by
example and moral influence, for the universal reign of human
liberty and the rights of man.*

No amount of argument, documentary evidence or papal
definitions will disabuse the hard-nosed Usan Catholic who has
been led to believe that such sentiments are compatible with the
Faith, for his utopian mentality is not the product of thinking. It
does not dwell in his intellect, for he has never been educated. Like
Pavlov's dog, he has been conditioned. He must be de-programmed
before he can be informed. He would profit more from the services
of a psychologist rather than those of a theologian or a historian.
What he needs most of all is contact with the living faith. For a start,
immersion in genuine liturgy would provide excellent therapy.

Usan Catholicism is not due to the Constitution. Nor can it be
blamed on godless government. It is rather the other way round. It
was Americanist Catholic education, supported by the liberal
Catholic media, which produced politicians like Al Smith, John and
Edward Kennedy and Mario Cuomo, and which produced the
Catholic voters who voted for them. One would normally expect
Catholic candidates to introduce the Catholic viewpoint into
politics, if not Catholic morality into government, but such has not
been the case. Quite the contrary. Al Smith, the first professed
Catholic to run for President, believed like Cardinal Newman that
Pius IX's *Syllabus of Errors* "had no dogmatic force." He was
therefore able to assure voters in 1928, "I believe in absolute
separation between Church and state ... I believe in the-support of
the public school." In 1933 he declared in Albany that "All the ills
of democracy can be cured by more democracy!"

A generation later, Kennedy, campaigning for the Presidency in
Houston, Texas, would protest, "I believe in an America where the
separation of Church and state is absolute ... where there is no
Catholic vote." In West Virginia he promised, "If any Pope
attempted to influence me as President, I would tell him it was
completely improper. If you took orders from the Pope you would
be breaking your oath of office and commit a sin against God."
Perhaps the apogee in inculturation was reached when he declared
in an interview for Look magazine in 1959, "Whatever one's
religion in his private life may be, to the officeholder nothing takes
precedence over his oath to uphold the Constitution and all its

parts." And we are all familiar with the position of New York's Governor Mario Cuomo, who declares himself personally opposed to abortion, but unwilling in conscience to interfere with anyone's constitutional rights to perform one or to undergo one.

Among Utopia's myriad errors, the most fundamental may lie in its concept of human liberty, the one on which it prides itself most, whereby liberty is viewed exclusively as freedom from constraint. Our blessed Lord during His life on earth never identified liberty with freedom from constraint. He said it was an effect of truth: "The truth shall make you free" (*John 8:32*).

If this be so, then how can a nation be "conceived in liberty" which is not first conceived in truth? And how can men be free where the truth itself is constrained and therefore unable to make them free? Divine light reveals the absurdity. Men who do not possess the truth, or only part of the truth, are morally enslaved to error. Christ the King, the supreme Ruler, tells us it is not government, nor liberty, nor equality, nor fraternity, but truth which confers, and then guarantees freedom.

This brings us to Pilate's question: "What is truth?" As Catholics we know it can only be that truth which is God himself, and which He has revealed to us through the Church He founded for that purpose. The United States has not been a free country at any time and is progressively less so, because it is not Catholic and does not place truth at the center of its political life. Truth has never been conferred on its citizens as public policy, as King Clovis, by political guarantees, conferred it on his Franks.

True, the Constitution has at no time acknowledged the universal Kingship of Christ according to the desires of the Sacred Heart, but it gave the Faith more than a sporting chance. By placing all religions on an equal level, the Bill of Rights placed no legal impediment to preaching the truth. Admittedly this is dangerous work, as the martyrology amply proves, but if the United States is not a Catholic nation today under the rule of Christ the King, the blame doesn't lie with the Constitution, much less with the occult forces which may have originally inspired it. Utopia is not to blame, nor the international bankers, nor Madelyn Murray O'Hare, nor secular humanism.

To blame is the phony Catholicism known as Americanism, which prepared the way for every so-called reform and innovation of Vatican II. Every Catholic who has knowingly subscribed to it is to blame, because its specious, self-serving accommodations to the monstrous political error called democracy have stifled the one thing that can make men free. By withholding the full truth from their fellow citizens, Usan Catholics stand guilty of the ultimate sin against fraternal charity. Crowning America's good with brotherhood from sea to shining sea profits little if the brothers aren't validly baptized and have no hope of eternal life.

Those who love their country and are aware of the deeply heretical nature of false Usan ideology have become a kind of subculture, not only in the land in which they were born, but even in their Church. To avoid full-fledged schizophrenia, about all they can do is take refuge in that life-saving Maurassian distinction between their real country and their legal country, between America and the United States. Like children of divorced parents, they must somehow manage to please both, holding to the one without despising the other. In other words, they must "render unto Caesar the things that are Caesar's and unto God the things that are God's" without slipping into serving two masters. The problem isn't new, and in the past martyrdom has sometimes proved the only viable solution.

THE VOICE OF THE DRAGON

To accomplish its lofty ends, Utopia sooner or later would have to dispose of its principal, indeed its only opponent, the Holy Catholic Church. It would, in other words, have to find some way to "dissolve Christ" (*1 John 4:3*). A movement to eliminate all faiths by forging them into one world religion consistent with the humanitarian ideals of Utopia had long been underway, growing clandestinely through the secret societies, and by the close of the 19th century Christianity had been sufficiently weakened for it to reveal itself. It was time for the second beast of the Apocalypse to make its public appearance. "Coming up out of the earth," it would look like a lamb with two horns, but it would speak with the voice of the dragon and "cause the earth and them that dwell therein to adore the first beast" (*Apo. 13:11-12*).

Through this false ecclesiastical agency, the Church would finally be subjected to Utopia. It was appropriate that the United States, the first of the purely secular man-made nations - one which had never formed part of Christendom - should provide the soil for its first formal proclamation. A great World Parliament of Religions was therefore called in 1893 in Chicago in an effort to explore and strengthen the common grounds of brotherhood which bind all men and which would make them truly one in mind and heart. That Catholic prelates were prevailed upon to participate in such an unprecedented conclave may have been the coup of the century.

Needless to say, Usan Catholics, born and bred in the land of freedom and equality, proved invaluable tools in bringing it about. Two years after the event, the spirit of prophecy descended on that staunch defender of the Faith, crusty Bernard McQuaid, Suffragan Bishop of Rochester. In a letter to Cardinal Ledochowski, Prefect of Propaganda in Rome, he delivered himself of the following:

> *Of late years, a spirit of liberalism is springing up in our body under such leaders as Mgr. Ireland and Mgr. Keane, that if not in our body under such leaders as Mgr. Ireland and Mgr. Keane, that if not checked in time, will bring disaster on the Church. Many a time Catholic laymen have remarked that the*

Catholic Church they once knew seems to be passing away, so greatly shocked are they at what they see passing around them.

We can only wonder what the good Bishop and these laymen would say at the sight of what is passing around us today. At the time Bishop McQuaid could not have gauged the enormity or longevity of the ecumania unleashed by the Parliament, which, although lasting only the seventeen days from September 11 to September 28, was the first of its kind in the history of the world and literally ushered in a new Christ for the new order of the ages. Recognizing in it, however, "every pretense of religious denomination from Mohammedanism and Buddhism to the lowest form of evangelicism and infidelity," his reaction was immediate. Unhampered by a collegiality not yet invented, he wound up denouncing Archbishop Ireland and his fellow Americanists roundly from the pulpit in his cathedral in November of the following year. His letter to Ledochowski had only been sent later by way of explanation.

Like most really dangerous temptations, the Parliament had arrived in an attractive, innocent looking package - a World's Fair put together to celebrate the quadricentenary of the discovery of America by the Catholic Christopher Columbus. Exhibits from America and the whole world were on display in Chicago's Jackson Park wherewith to dazzle the eyes of the most sophisticated visitor. And no eyes were more dazzled than those of the bombastic Archbishop of St. Paul, John Ireland, as they scanned so monumental a testimony to human progress:

Hither shall be brought the products of labor and of art, the treasures of earth and of sea, the inventions of this wondrously inventive century, the fruits of learning and genius. The whole globe is astir in preparation to fill to repletion the palaces we have erected. The invitation has been sent forth in all the fullness and warmth of the heart of this republic, and the nations of the world have harkened to it as never before they harkened to a voice calling men to exposition. The best that America owns, the best that the world can bring, will now be seen in Jackson Park !

To hear Ireland tell it:

> *The Exposition of Chicago will show forth the results of the discovery of Columbus. In this wise Columbus is honored. What Columbus gave to the world was not only the America of the year 1492 ... What he gave was the America of the year 1892. What Columbus gave was, in a large measure, the marvelous progress of modern times!*

Viewed in such perspective, it's not surprising that the Columbian Exposition found many enthusiastic supporters in the Church, Leo XIII among them. Upon the request of the U.S. government, he saw no difficulty about lending for display some valuable fifteenth century maps from the Vatican, which arrived in the hands of Archbishop Francesco Satolli, his personal representative to the Fair. Although in those days of overt anti-Catholic sentiment Satolli could enjoy no diplomatic standing, the Pope seized this auspicious occasion to appoint him the first permanent Apostolic Delegate to the American hierarchy and to found an Apostolic Delegation in the nation's capital. The Leonine encyclical on Columbus was furthermore pronounced at the Fair.

+

The Exposition was originally planned as a purely secular event, limited to professional groups and merchants of material progress. The idea of an auxiliary Congress of Religions seems to have hatched in the mind of a Swedenborgian lawyer prominent in Chicago civic affairs, one Charles C. Bonney, who believed the Fair should present aspects of spiritual progress also. As head of his Congress Auxiliary, he appointed a committee composed of representative Christians and Jews, with Archbishop Ireland as one of its members, to launch the project. Its Chairman was the Presbyterian Rev. J.H. Barrows. Needless to say, the ambience was predominantly liberal Protestant.

Inasmuch as religion was so important a factor in human development, as these divines put it, it was eventually decided that the Congress should be open to all the religions of the world. Some three thousand invitations were issued forthwith, which elicited mixed reactions. The Archbishop of Canterbury was indignant:

Given "that the Christian religion is the one religion ... I do not understand how that religion can be regarded as a member of a

Parliament of Religions, without assuming the equality of other intended members and the parity of their position and claims." Gladstone was skeptical, and the Sultan of Turkey unconvinced. Catholic conservatives in the U.S. were, like McQuaid, horrified. So were many Protestants.

There were, however, very many acceptances from all denominations and a good number from the eastern Asian sects, who had always proved inspiring to the "Yankee Hindus" among the New England Transcendentalists. Scholars active in the field of comparative religion, like Max Muller, were of course especially supportive. Some minor religious groups who felt misunderstood looked forward to having their say. Theosophists responded with alacrity. They and others looked upon the Congress as a missionary opportunity, and Americanists, alas, were foremost in this category.

Delegated to sell the American Catholic Archbishops on the idea at their annual meeting in New York, Bishop Keane pled, "It is not in our power to hinder the Parliament from taking place. It is already certain that all the other great forms of religion will be ably represented. Can the Catholic Church afford not to be there?" The Archbishops thought not, and instructed him to select twenty Catholic speakers to expound Catholic doctrine at the Congress.

To its directors Keane wrote:

> *It is only by a friendly and brotherly comparison of convictions that reasonable men can ever come to an agreement about the all-important truths which are the foundation of religion, and that an end can be put to the religious divisions and antagonisms which are a grief to our Father in Heaven. Such an assemblage of intelligent and conscientious men, presenting their religious convictions without minimizing, without acrimony, without controversy, with love and truth and humanity, will be an honorable event in the history of religion and cannot fail to accomplish much good.*

Thus would Americanism in the space of a few days accomplish what Holy Mother Church had not been able to do in two thousand years of suffering and warfare.

Besides the general assembly, there were numerous subsidiary Congresses, each putting on its own show for its own members both before and after the general Parliament. Nearly every religious denomination was represented, from the Church of England to Jains and Zoroastrians, even evolutionists and psychical researchers. There was a sizeable scientific sector, which believed in promoting mutual understanding by historical and scientific investigation of the various religions and relating them to the concerns of the world. Most significant was a Women's Congress, where Julia Ward Howe, Elizabeth Stanton, Frances Willard and other well-known feminists of the day told their side of it. Annie Besant, star of the American Theosophical Society was of their number. There was even a token lady minister, the Rev. Dr. Augusta Chapin of Chicago, who proclaimed prophetically that when it carne to women's freedom, "We are still at the dawn of this new era!"

The Catholics also had their own Congress, to which the Pope sent a special blessing via Cardinal Gibbons. Actually it was the successor to the Catholic Congress convened in Baltimore the previous year for the centennial of the establishment of the American hierarchy. There it had been decided that the next meeting would be held in Chicago in conjunction with the World's Fair. It took for its theme "the social question," suggested by Leo XIII's recent encyclical *On the Condition of Labor* and was directed to an assessment of Catholic progress in the new world.

The official welcome to the Catholic gathering was given by the aforementioned Swedenborgian, Charles Bonney, who noted, "That a great change has come in the relations of the Catholic Church and the Protestant churches with each other is known throughout the world." Indeed. Rev. Barrows afterwards declared that he felt that "the most imposing of all the denominational Congresses was that held by the Catholic Church." All in all, much of its proceedings could be summed up in Archbishop Ireland's exultant, "The Gospel in one hand and the Constitution of the United States in the other!"

+

Attendance at the general interfaith Congress was so overflowing there was a flourishing black market in tickets by the closing session. Altogether it is said to have attracted some 140,000 people. Over four thousand crammed themselves into the great Hall of Columbus for the grand opening, where the central position on the platform was accorded Cardinal Gibbons. Proclaiming that, "We appeal only to the tribunal of conscience and of intellect," he gave the "universal blessing" and throughout the proceedings used the Protestant version of the Our Father. With him at the speakers table were an increasingly uncomfortable Archbishop Satolli, although he spoke no English, flanked by Bishop Keane, Archbishop Ireland, Archbishops Feehan and Ryan of Chicago and Philadelphia and other prominent members of the hierarchy, all basking in a gratifying acceptance usually denied Catholics in Protestant America. Whether agree with or not, Archbishop Ireland's thunderous oratory drew record crowds.

In order to avoid any shadow of controversy which might mar the ecumenical spirit, no public discussion was permitted after the prepared speeches, although questions could be put to the speakers afterwards. In all justice, it must be admitted that some excellent presentations of Catholic doctrine were made. Cardinal Gibbons stated flat-footedly in his opener that he really wasn't searching for truth at all, like most of the Parliament, "for by the grace of God, I am conscious that I have found it." Bishop Keane spoke on the Incarnation in history and on "The Ultimate Religion." The Paulist Fathers Walter Elliott and Augustine Hewitt were in their glory, the latter favoring the assembly with "A Rational Demonstration of the Being of God." Mgr. Seton of Newark spoke on Scripture. All apparently sincerely believed that they had found at last the real method for converting the Protestant U.S.A. to the true faith. Eventually, they were sure, Rome would have to acknowledge the superiority of their Americanist approach to apologetics.

But the worm was in the apple. The Jesuit Fr. Thomas Sherman of St. Louis assured his motley listeners that every Catholic must always follow his conscience, even if this meant sometimes contradicting the Pope. The Maryland-born Francis Redwood, become an archbishop from Australia, maintained, "I do not pretend as a Catholic to have the whole truth ... I can appreciate, love and esteem any element of truth found outside that body of truth." Later, Bishop Keane was convinced that, "Nearly every sentence during those seventeen days tended to show that positive doctrinal differences which had held Christians apart during three centuries are fast being obliterated." The Paulist Catholic World hit the nail on the head by calling the Parliament "a great love feast of the brotherhood of man."

When it was all over, the Catholic liberals proudly presented a special edition of the Parliament proceedings - which, even selected and condensed, ran to over a thousand pages - to Pope Leo; and Cardinal Gibbons wrote to Cardinal Rampolla, Vatican Secretary of State, to explain the rationale behind their participation. They nonetheless awaited repercussions from Rome.

Bishop Keane, writing his Americanist friend Bishop Denis O'Connell at the American College there, said he believed Archbishop Satolli "looks askance at our part in the Parliament of Religions, as do no doubt all the conservatives ... I am confident that the result is an enormous advantage to the Church. But I take it for granted that I shall be denounced for it."

The pope, alarmed not only at what he was hearing from his new Apostolic Delegate, but also from Bishop McQuaid and many others both lay and clerical in the U.S., reacted accordingly in due time. In January 1895 he issued the encyclical *Longinqua Oceani*, slapping the Americanists' wrists for their unqualified support of the principle of separation of church and state. Then, in a letter dated the following September, he flatly forbade any future Catholic participation in any gathering resembling that indulged in in Chicago. He advised Catholics to hold their own conferences, to which non-Catholics might be allowed, but only as auditors. This was followed by an article in *Civiltu Cattolica* denouncing the Neopelagianism which allegedly inspired the Parliament. Bishop McQuaid was gratified, but as he wrote to his friend Archbishop Corrigan, the Americanists "can never repair the harm done in the past."

Finally there appeared in 1899 *Testem Benevolentiae*, condemning Americanism outright.

+

Adding his mite to the wealth of benign platitudes spoken at the Parliament, Archbishop Feehan had remarked happily, "No matter how we differ in faith or in religion, there is one thing that is common to us all, and that is a common humanity." At this date, a century later, this is still all the religions of the world have in common, but with a new twist. The serpent had been invited in, and as the oratory rolled through session after session, it was quietly laying its eggs. There were time bombs and sleepers in the World

Parliament of Religions, just as later there would be in the Second Vatican Council.

Protestants and Catholics, concentrating on what they thought was basically their own private show for whitewashing and/or reconciling their differences, must have accepted as self evident the judgment of the Parliament's historian that the event "has shown conclusively that the only worthy idea of God is monotheism; that the belief in a divine revelation was a necessary step to religious unity, and that ... as long as God is God and man is man, Jesus Christ is the center of religion forever." Little did they suspect that Christianity itself would soon be floundering and fighting for its life in the narcotic embrace of the eastern mysticism they had so cordially but rather condescendingly admitted to their Parliament of Religions. Yet they should have known, for all the signs were there.

Although he drew large audiences and held them spellbound, Archbishop Ireland was not the only star of the show. A greater, it turns out, was the brilliant Bengali Swami Vivekananda, who was attractively set off by two lesser lights: Anagarika Dharrnapala from Singala, who founded the Mahabodhi Society for the revitalization of Buddhism, and the Japanese Zen Buddhist Shaku Soen, who a mere ten years later would found the first Zen monastery in America. These were the first authoritative apostles of their traditions to travel to the West and to be officially received.

At the close of the Congress, one of their group, Protup Chunder Mozoomdar, leader of the east Indian Brahmo-Somaj sect, explained how for him the kingdom of heaven was "a vast concentric circle with various circumferences of doctrines, authorities and organizations from outer to inner, from inner to inner still, until heaven and earth become one." Here was the New Way, brought to us at long last, right to our doorstep, from the mystic East, which promised to solve all of Christianity's ecumenical difficulties easily and quickly, without controversy or altercation of any kind, simply by evaporating them. The old Christ who promised the sword of division and the Cross to those who would follow Him in this life, must give way to the peaceful cosmic Christ of the New Age, who promises Nirvana now, rolling in on Buddha's eternal wheel. One trip to India and its slums - where the fruits of such "religion" are plain to see - should be sufficient to dispel so gigantic a temptation, but not to the blind ecumenist.

Vivekananda, a former law student whom the *New York Times* referred to as "undoubtedly the greatest figure in the Parliament of Religions," was heir to the mantle of the great syncretist saint Sri Ramakrishna Paramahansa, who had died only six years previously. In India he still shares supreme honors with Gandhi on its postage stamps, all the while enjoying the highest esteem among the "enlightened" there and the world over. As founder of the Ramakrishna Mission, the charismatic Vivekananda is responsible for the proliferation throughout the West of those outposts of intellectual Hinduism known as Vedanta Societies, whose influence by now has literally permeated the secular world and a significant part of the religious with Ramakrishna's teachings.

Tal Brooke, in *When the World Will Be as One*, says of him:

Vivekananda was an inspired orator whose pleas for unity became irresistible to the thousands attending the World Parliament of Religions. Anyone who condemned the spiritual treasures of this noble figure from the East was simply exhibiting those 'narrow- minded biases' typical of Western Christian' culture ... Here began the early traces of today's common cultural anthropological argument which defines different religions as being universal spiritual truths filtered through variant grids of culture and tradition. Spiritual truths could now be seen as wearing the clothing of a given culture's language and imagery. So what the world needed were religious pundits acting as transcultural interpreters of religion.

... Vivekananda's command of rhetoric and apparent nobility and virtue of character won his case time and again. Beneath it all was the admonition: 'All roads lead to God'." In this he simply propounded the message of his old guru Ramakrishna, who had studied the world's religions and boasted that he had reached samadhi, i.e., enlightenment in every one of them. Christ, Buddha, Krishna or whoever, what did it matter? All, he revealed, had led him equally to the godhead. When his disciple addressed the opening of the Congress with, "Sisters and Brothers of America," his audience was startled, but now, a century later, we have all gotten used to it, even at the Holy Sacrifice of the Mass. "I am proud," said he, "to belong to a religion that has taught the

world both tolerance and acceptance. We believe not only in
universal toleration, but we accept all religions to be true.

+

The World Parliament of Religions cast very long shadows. It
would be impossible to catalogue all it spawned in false hopes,
indifferentism, moral apathy and general confusion. After a
hundred years, feminism is rampant, bidding fair to destroy the
home and human society as we know it, and there is hardly a
seminary or school of secondary education that isn't wallowing in
comparative religion. It would be tedious - indeed impossible -
merely to list the inter-faith groups, active and flourishing
worldwide on both the national and international levels, which have
been put together on the pattern first set by the pioneer Parliament
in Chicago.

In 1901 an International Congress on the history of religions
opened in Paris, followed over the years by many others in various
European capitals. Marking the fiftieth anniversary of the Chicago
Parliament, a World Fellowship of Faiths met again in Chicago and
New York in 1933-4. The special hymn composed for its closing
ceremony tells it all:

One Cosmic Brotherhood,
One Universal Good,
One Source, One Sway.
One Law Beholding Us,
One Purpose Molding Us,
One Life Enfolding Us,
In Love Always.

In 1936 a World Congress of Faiths was established in London,
whose journal, *World Faiths*, has been published since 1946. After
World War II the movement gained fresh impetus and culminated
in the establishment of the well-known World Council of Churches
in Amsterdam in 1948, all Christian denominations lending it their
membership except for Catholics, Southern Baptists and Missouri
Synod Lutherans. Here may be mentioned the Baha'ists, a world
assembly of religions founded in Persia in 1844 as a heretical
Moslem sect, predating the American Parliament. They established

their main center on Mt. Carmel in 1953 and now have a huge temple in the U.S. near Chicago at Wilmette. Needless to say, the birth centenary of Vivekananda could not be forgotten. It was celebrated internationally in Calcutta in 1963.

After the U.S. Inter-Religious Conference on Peace, held in Washington, D.C. in 1966, at which the American Cardinal John Wright was present, interfaith efforts had become permanently indentured to the peace movement. By this time studying one another's "histories" in an effort to reach a "better understanding" was far behind us. The great Kyoto Conference in 1970 dealt mainly with "the practical impact of religion on world affairs," with stress on "interdependence" - Catholic Archbishop Angelo Fernandes of New Delhi presiding. Kyoto hatched the World Conference of Religion for Peace which was accredited that same year to the U.N. through the Office of Public Information. The WCRP works regularly through that international body, besides countless national subsidiaries. Now no place on earth is safe from dialogue, ecumenism and irenicism. There was a conference in Nairobi by 1975, and another in Chiang Mai, Thailand by 1977. A conference to spark a Global Congress held forth in Boston in 1978. Today everyone is in the act, even the Dalai Lama of Tibet.

The United States, where inter-faithery was formally declared, has remained in the forefront ever since. In 1959 an American woman from Greenwich, Connecticut by the name of Judith Hollister, a dabbler in theology, conceived the idea of providing one great building for its permanent use. First contacting the Ford Foundation, she was eventually directed to Eleanor Roosevelt, whose enthusiastic help she enlisted at a tea "where the whole room was filled with beards and turbans." With letters of introduction from the First Lady, Mrs. Hollister was soon meeting with key international religious leaders here and abroad to turn the architect's plans into reality.

Seven years later twenty acres on the Potomac River near Washington, D.C. were dedicated as the proposed site. In 1967, at a special audience, Pope Paul VI promised the lady he would pray for "*il Templo delia Compresione,*" this name for the edifice - the Temple of Understanding - having been adopted at the suggestion of Mrs. Ellsworth Bunker, wife of the then American Ambassador to India. The project, supported by celebrities as diverse as Margaret Mead and Robert McNamara, is still very much alive. An international fellowship was created, and an ambitious series of "Spiritual Summit Conferences" was embarked on. To date these have been held for the most part on prestigious college campuses and in historic churches here and abroad.

+

During and after the Second Vatican Council, the Catholic clergy and laity began indulging in ever more unbridled religious cooperation with groups outside the Church, following the lead of Cardinals Bea and Suenens in the heady intellectual atmosphere created by Teilhard de Chard in. For their authorization, these seized on the Council's Declaration *Nostra Aetate* to the effect that, "all peoples comprise a single community," and that:

> *The Church, therefore, has this exhortation for her sons; prudently and lovingly, through dialogue and collaboration with the followers of other religions, and in witness of Christian faith and life, acknowledge, preserve and promote the spiritual and moral goods found among these men, as well as the values in their society and culture.*

Seeking to carry out these directives, Pope Paul VI established a special Secretariat for Non-Christians, "so that," he told the Sacred College:

> *...there shall be a means of coming to some kind of dialogue, both considerate and faithful, with all those who still believe in God and adore him. With the help of this initial step and of yet others, we intend to make a clear demonstration of the Catholic dimension of the Church which, at this time, and in this conciliar atmosphere, not only embraces in the bonds of understanding, friendship and fraternal consideration those who are inside the Church, but once more looks outside to find some basis for dialogue and contact with all souls of good will.*

Speaking in Calcutta at the First Spiritual Summit Conference sponsored by the aforementioned Temple of Understanding, the Trappist-turned-Buddhist monk Thomas Merton was one to cut through what he considered such unnecessary red tape: "My dear brothers," he assured his hearers, "we are already one, but we imagine that we are not. What we have to recover is our original unity. What we have to be is what we already are!"

By now the utopian virus is so widespread in the Church as to occasion little surprise. No one raised an eyebrow when Fr. Robert Fox, editor of the *Fatima Family Messenger*, knelt publicly for the blessing of the Orthodox Patriarch of Corinth. Archbishop Lustiger of Paris, addressing French Canadian students at Laval University in Montreal on "*Belief in the Modern World*," told them:

> *It seems to me that the new world is only beginning. I call new world not only America, but also this New Age into which humanity is entering. We are only at the beginning of the Christian era! ... Man's condition as creature is his highest dignity: that's the foundation of the Rights of Man!, etc. etc.*

In some ways, the most disturbing image of the New Age Christian is projected by the little Albanian nun Mother Teresa, Foundress of the Missionaries of Charity. Enjoying worldwide acclaim for her work among the poor, she has been awarded numerous worldly honors, the American Medal of Freedom and the Nobel Peace Prize among them. In 1975 Time magazine didn't hesitate to canonize her as "a living saint" in a cover story, for the new utopian world could not fail to love her. She speaks only of love and peace, and adopted the Indian sari unhesitatingly as a universal religious habit for her nuns, who in their chapels are wont to remove their shoes at prayer and assume the lotus position in their meditations. Their silent, smiling propaganda has seeped through nearly every major city of the world. At the order's Queen of Peace Home for pregnant women in Washington, D.C., for instance, co-workers are permitted to teach yoga exercises.

Best of all, from the world's point of view, is that little Mother Teresa doesn't try to convert anyone to the Faith, not even on their deathbeds. According to a Washington Post article on the foundation she made in the nation's capital, "As for the human beings she cares for, she does not chalk up converts for Jesus at the last minute. Dying Hindus are given Hindu ceremonies if they request them. Buddhists are accorded Buddhist rites," and so presumably with all denominations. Mother Teresa stresses only that "We are all children of God!" Regardless of religious persuasions, "He's going to say the same thing to everybody: 'Children, come forth to be judged.'"

Mother Teresa does, however, ardently seek converts to a favorite apostolate, and that is Natural Family Planning, that age-old Manichaean practice of birth prevention known to St. Augustine. She is adamantly opposed to abortion and other forms of birth control, but not to this one. Quoting an Associated Press story, a Catholic Register special supplement reported that her planning program "has prevented more than 1.1 million unwanted births in [India] during the past 11 years." ... Her "sisters make weekly repeat visits to families who adopt the program to record the results. Mother Teresa credited the program with preventing 100,000 births a year throughout India ... A United Nations team recently made a three-year study of the program to check results, and called its effectiveness remarkable."

In her acceptance speech for the Nobel Prize in December 1979, which she opened with St. Francis' Prayer for Peace, she openly boasted of doing a "thing which is very beautiful - we are teaching our beggars, our leprosy patients, our slum dwellers, our people of the street, natural family planning. And in Calcutta alone in six years ... we have had 61,273 babies less from the families who would have had, but because they practice this natural way of abstaining." Is this the voice of a Catholic? Or is it the voice of the dragon speaking as the utopian Christ planning his new society among the "disadvantaged?" For this and her other endeavors, Mother Teresa is a brilliant money raiser. In the same speech, thanking her Norwegian auditors for their financial support, she added, "I don't want you to give me from your abundance. I want that you give me until it hurts." Thus is the hallowed old Christian vocabulary, with all its beautiful evangelical overtones, put into the service of the sociological Jesus, the "lamb with two horns," who" executes all the power of the former beast in his sight" (*Apo. 13:12*)

THE POLITICAL DIMENSION OF SACRED HEART DEVOTION

Catholic devotion to the Sacred Heart of its Lord, mightily prefigured in the Old Covenant with Israel, emerged into full view, theologically and palpably, in the bloody scene we call the Crucifixion. When Longinus plunged his spear into the Sacred Body publicly exposed on the Cross, he struck the heart of a King. There could be no mistake, for the sign above the thorn-crowned Head of the Man enthroned on the Cross read plainly, "Jesus of Nazareth, King of the Jews."

The political symbolism in that scene is beyond human contrivance. With one powerful, predestined blow, Longinus, effective agent of the secular authority, "opened" (says St. John) the royal side, and the fountain of Blood and water which gushed forth continues to this day unto the sanctification of all this King's willing subjects. Devotion to His Sacred Heart is therefore no sentimental devotion to be pursued only in private. Essentially, it is a political commitment. The Sacred Heart of Christ the King is source and center of the Christian state, human manifestation of the divine Monarchy from which all monarchy takes its name. Its temporal dimensions extend into eternity.

Only when viewed from this perspective can the true purpose of Sacred Heart devotion be discerned. Otherwise it is simply a super-excellent practice among many others designed by God to bring the individual into greater intimacy with Him. Sacred Heart devotion does this, to be sure, but its objective is ultimately and fundamentally political in the real sense of the word politics. It was forged by the divine Wisdom to bring not only the individual, but whole nations into intimacy with God.

Needless to say, the devotion was never preached in such terms in the USA, where democracy reigns supreme and separation of Church and state is dogma. It was deemed too dangerous if not outright subversive. We were led to believe that God, whose name the U.S. Constitution does not mention, is not really interested in politics anyway, and that religion is a purely private matter. As a consequence, most of us are familiar only with the requests which our Lord made to St. Margaret Mary Alacoque regarding the nine

First Fridays of reparation and the institution of the Feast of the Sacred Heart.

No doubt we reaped immense spiritual profit from the devotion without being acquainted with the political framework in which the apparitions took place at Paray-le-Monial, and without being aware of the political necessity which had dictated them. Even Pius XII in his masterly encyclical on the Sacred Heart, *Haurieiis Aquas*, published in 1956 for the centenary of the institution of the Feast, dwells almost exclusively on the spiritual, personal character of the devotion. Although he prescribes it as the best antidote for the ills of society "such as cause," says he, "sharp conflict among individuals, families, nations and the whole world," he presents it primarily as a super-eminent religious practice efficaciously rooted in charity.

Not that St. Margaret Mary was the first to receive communications from the Sacred Heart. The first recorded vision of the Sacred Heart was to St. Lutgarde in the 13th century, but as we have noted, the devotion actually began in the Gospels, particularly in that of St. John, who was privileged to lean familiarly on the breast of our Lord at the Last Supper and who witnessed the opening of the divine Heart on the Cross. As early as the third century, meditation on the piercing of Christ's side was regularly practiced by the devout every afternoon at three o'clock.

Patristic theologians like Origen, St. Augustine, St. Hippolytus, St. Justin Martyr and St. Cyprian established the devotion on firm doctrinal ground, and it thrived among the great mystics of the middle ages. Among these were St. Anselm of Canterbury, St. Bernard, St. Francis, St. Margaret of Cortona, St. Mechtilde, St. Angela of Foligno, St. Bonaventure, St. Catherine of Siena, St. Albert the Great, St. Bridget and many others. "Little Hours of the Glorious Heart of Jesus Christ" were recited in Cologne. Religious Orders - Carthusians, Franciscans, Benedictines and Dominicans - produced whole schools of spirituality based on the wounded heart of the Savior. A feast of the Holy Lance was approved by Pope Innocent VI for the second Friday after Easter, and by the end of the 15th century a proper feast of the Sacred Heart was observed by the Dominicans of Alsace.

St. Gertrude of Helfta left voluminous literature on the Sacred Heart, but she had been told by St. John that divine wisdom was reserving the fullness of the devotion for the last days, when it would be especially needed, "that the world that is growing old and whose love is weakening may be revived." So it's not surprising that so many counter-Reformation saints became ardent propagators, even before the revelations to St. Margaret Mary.

It was the French priest St. John Eudes, apostle of the Immaculate Heart of Mary, who first directed modern piety to the Heart of her Son. Called by St. Pius X "initiator, teacher and apostle of the liturgical cult of the Sacred Heart," he succeeded in establishing on solid theological ground what until then had been a widespread pious cult. In 1672 he obtained ecclesiastical approval for a Mass of the Sacred Heart for celebration in his own Order, the Congregation of Jesus and Mary.

The very next year, on the feast of St. John the Apostle, December 27, 1673, began the series of four great apparitions of the Sacred Heart to St. Margaret Mary in the convent of the Visitation at Paray-le-Monial in France. In them converged explosively all the communications the Sacred Heart had ever made to His Church. They were concerned with love, divine love, and with the love God expected from men in return. This was nothing new, for this theme runs throughout the Old Testament as well as the New.

+

What seemed to be totally new in the revelations to St. Margaret Mary is the political dimension of Sacred Heart devotion. So obvious in the scenario on Calvary, this aspect seems to have all but disappeared from view until it reappeared suddenly in 1689, when the Sacred Heart entrusted the young nun with a special message for the King of France. Already, at our Lord's request, she had been expiating Louis XIV's personal aberrations. The King had been entirely converted as a result of her sufferings, and was spending his golden years with his morganatic wife Mme. de Maintenon in exemplary piety. Although the new religious atmosphere at court was openly resented by its more worldly members, His Majesty persevered, and is said to have died the death of a saint.

The substance of our Lord's message had been conveyed in six letters written by St. Margaret Mary, five of them to her former Superior, Mother de Saumaise, and the last one to her Jesuit spiritual director, Fr. Croiset. The second letter, dated June 17,

1689, begins by speaking of some great political designs of our Lord:

> *... which can be executed only by His almighty power ... It seems to me He wishes to enter with pomp and magnificence into the homes of princes and kings so as to be honored there to the same degree that He was outraged, despised and humiliated in His Passion, and to receive as much pleasure on seeing the world's great ones reduced and humbled before Him as He felt bitterness on seeing himself reduced to nothing at their feet.*
>
> *And here are the words I heard regarding our King: 'Inform the eldest son of My Sacred Heart that ... he will secure his birth into grace and glory by the consecration he will make of himself to My adorable Heart ... and through his mediation, that of the great ones of the earth. He (the Sacred Heart) wishes to reign in his palace, to be painted on his standards and to be graven on his arms to render them victorious over all his enemies, by bringing these proud, arrogant heads under his heel and effect his triumph over all the enemies of the Church.'*

There were other requests. In the saint's fifth letter, dated August 28 of the same year, she says our Lord desired a building to be erected in which would be displayed an image of the divine Heart, to which the King and his entire court would formally consecrate themselves. The King, furthermore, chosen by our Lord as "His faithful friend," was to ensure that a special Mass in His honor would be authorized by the Holy See and a formal cultus established. In return the King was promised divine protection against his "enemies, both visible and invisible." It is now known that these invisible enemies were the occult forces of Freemasonry set into motion by the "merchants of light." Already they had crossed the Channel from England and were gathering strength in France.

And speaking of channels, our Lord made it clear that the Jesuit Fr. de la Chaize, Louis XIV's confessor, had been chosen by God to see to the execution of His designs. "By virtue of the power He had given him over the heart of our great King," wrote St. Margaret Mary, "the success of the matter depended on him."

Incredible as it may seem, scholars like Fr. Guitton, S.J., who wrote on the matter in the *Revue d'Ascétique et de Mystique,*

(July-Sept. 1958), have now determined with near certainty that Fr. de la Chaize never relayed these messages to the King, and whatever consecrations may have been made were done only privately and did not fulfill the required conditions. Fr. de la Chaize's reasons are still not clear, but he acted deliberately, perhaps for lack of authorization from the Father General of the Society of Jesus. The General, Fr. Thyrsus Gonzalez de Santalla, was known to be formally hostile to the devotion, for he censured and banished the saint's director Fr. Croiset for having written an account of the revelations.

We are confronted by a mystery of iniquity. Following the lead of Benedict XIV, even the Papacy for a long time refused to establish a Feast of the Sacred Heart for the universal Church, and it was not until the reign of Pius IX that the cult of the Sacred Heart was accorded liturgical status.

The tradition of the French Visitation nuns holds it for certain that Louis XIV did nevertheless learn of the desires of the Sacred Heart through other sources. One was England's dethroned queen Maria Beatrice, who had taken refuge with the nuns in France. Louis XIV was already practicing the devotion as preached by St. John Eudes, to whom he had allocated 2000 pounds for France's first chapel to be dedicated to the Sacred Heart.

Undoubtedly he would have submitted St. Margaret Mary's requests to his spiritual director for approval, with a view to acting on them, but evidently the response was negative, and he obeyed his director. Thus, in strict justice, the King must be absolved of personal blame for the consequences, which proved to be not only disastrous for France, but for the whole world. We suffer them today.

+

The divine communications had been directed to Louis XIV's person, but not to him as an individual. Had this been the case the extraordinary means used would have been entirely disproportionate. It was Louis as King who was addressed. Fr. Bainvel, theologian of the Sacred Heart, writes:

> *The three objects of the message: the church, the consecration, the flag are by their very nature national, durable*

and perpetual; the triumph over the enemies of God and the Church resulting from the accomplishment of the message, is even more national, inasmuch as it involves the whole future of France and her providential Catholic mission, her vocation and her raison d' être.

In the person of the King all his successors and the nation itself are addressed. The entire court was to take part in the consecration. God's gifts being without repentance, no time limit was set, and presumably God still waits.

But why the King of France? Why not some other monarch, perhaps even one more worthy? The answer lies ultimately in the divine predilection, but proximately it lies in the fact that under the new dispensation of grace, the French kings are the new line of David, eldest sons of the Sacred Heart, rulers of the "eldest daughter of the Church." A long and venerable tradition supports this belief. Pope Gregory IX as it were canonized it when he wrote in a famous letter to the King St. Louis:

> *France is God's very kingdom ... The enemies of France are the enemies of Christ ... The tribe of Judah was the prefiguration of the kingdom of France ... The Redeemer chose the blessed kingdom of France as special executive of His divine will.*

There has been unexpected corroboration of this in modern times. In 1972 a confidant and part-time secretary to Padre Pio wrote several letters to a friend in religion in which he related what the holy Capuchin had told him on this subject. Excerpted by the Marquis de la Franquerie in Ascendances Davidiques des Rois de France, these read in part:

> *Padre used to tell me that without the support of the royal power of David, the Church falls into decadence, overpowered by the spirit of the serpent which is raising its proud head over the head of the Church. Padre Pio used to say that the royal power is a divine power which fells serpents. Republics on the other hand raise the serpents' spirits, who sacrifice God's people, preventing them from aspiring heavenwards to God ... This is Europe's problem today under the republics.*

Again:

> *Padre Pio knew that in France is hidden a power which will reveal itself at the appointed hour ... Only the royal power, the one God gave David, is capable of ruling governments. Without David's royal power, properly recognized and in place ... the Christian religion does not have the indispensable support it needs to uphold the truth of God's word ... God's power no longer resides in the hearts of ministers and heads of state. How great will be the world's misfortune before men understand this truth!*

We must remember that Christendom proper did not begin with the conversion of Constantine. Decisive as this was, the Roman Empire had remained basically pagan in political concept, despite a Christian head and a preponderantly Christian population. It was an empire based on human justice. From the Cross God proclaimed an empire based on love. Politically, as we have seen, Christendom began with the baptism of Clovis, King of the Salk Franks, a monarch who, like Constantine, owed his conversion to a divinely accorded military victory. Under the influence of Queen Clothilde and the Catholic Bishop of Reims, St. Remi, Clovis promised to become a Christian in return for the defeat of the Alemani at Tolbiac.

In gratitude he dictated a constitution whose opening words are "The Illustrious Nation of the Franks, having God himself for Founder" and which formally recognizes France as perpetual preserve of Christ the King. This was the new Israel, the first nation on earth to be founded from its inception on Christian principles. Praying that "the Lord Jesus Christ direct those who govern it in the paths of piety," the document closed with, "Long live Christ who loves the Franks! Long live the King of the Franks, who is Christ's Lieutenant!"

According to Hincmar, Archbishop of Reims, the Baptism of Clovis and his subjects on Christmas Day, 496, was marked by a supernatural manifestation. The Church was suddenly filled with dazzling light and a voice was heard saying, "Peace be to you! It is I. Be not afraid. Persevere in My favor!" Whereupon St. Remi, filled with the spirit of prophecy, turned to the King with these words:

> *Know, my son, that the Kingdom of France is predestined by God for the defense of the Roman Church, which is the only true Church of Christ. This Kingdom will one day be greater than all Kingdoms and will embrace the outer limits of the Roman Empire ... It will last to the end of time ... It will be victorious as long as it is faithful to the Roman faith. But it will be severely chastised whenever it is faithless to its vocation.*

The similarity of these words to those God so many times addressed to ancient Israel is very striking.

Clovis' coronation proved equally extraordinary. According to Hincmar:

> *On entering the Baptistry, the cleric bearing the chrism found himself separated by the crowd from the one officiating and was unable to reach him. The Holy Chrism was lacking. The priest therefore raised his eyes to heaven, begging the Lord to help him in this pressing necessity. Suddenly there appeared flying near his hand, before the eyes of the delighted and astonished crowd, a white dove bearing in its bill a phial of Holy Oil whose scent perfumed all those present with a fragrance unutterable.*

A venerable tradition avers that this miraculous Chrism was always used thereafter to anoint the French kings, and them alone, other monarchs being consecrated only with the oil of catechumens as specified in the Roman Pontifical. To this Chrism is attributed the miraculous power received by Clovis at his coronation to cure scrofula and other ills. It descended to his legitimate successors, who used it effectively provided they were in a state of grace. This royal charism is acknowledged by no less a person than St. Thomas Aquinas in *De regimine principum*, not to mention Pope Paul III, who in a Bull dated January 1548, refers to the French king's "holy unction and the power of curing the sick."

In view of these antecedents, the king of France was, in a manner of speaking, a sort of bishop in the temporal order, where political sovereignty is what Holy Orders is in the spiritual order. Even in modern times, popes have acknowledged the quasi-sacred character of the French monarchy. One was St. Pius X, who told Cardinal Lucon, Archbishop of Rheims in 1907:

> *The Baptism of Clovis marked the birth of a great nation: the Tribe of Judah of the New Era, which always prospered as long as she was faithful to orthodoxy, as long as she maintained the union of the Priesthood with the government, as long as she proved herself, not in word, but in act, the Eldest Daughter of the Church.*

Divine Providence raised up the barbarian Frankish nation within the Roman Empire to purify it of its Arian and pagan dross and make it truly Christian. "With French civilization was born Catholic, Apostolic, Roman civilization," called French, says the Abbe Vial, "only because France carried the torch! ... France took as her foundation the very cornerstone of the Church: Christ. Small wonder she benefited from the universality of Christ and the Church." Her fidelity to Christ earned her the glories of St. Charlemagne and St. Louis.

When later she lapsed from grace and her very existence as a nation was threatened, God intervened by sending St. Joan of Arc to deliver her. It is well known how Joan defeated the English pretender, restored a doubting Charles VII to his throne and was burned at the stake for her trouble. The essence of her mission, however, was revitalizing the pact of Tolbiac originally made between our Lord and His Lieutenant the King of France. She accomplished this by insisting on the coronation and anointing of Charles at Reims according to the ancient tradition.

That done, the famous triple donation took place. She asked the King to hand over his palace to her along with his newly recovered kingdom, so that she might then formally return France to Christ. The grateful King agreed, and both transactions were drawn up and publicly notarized. Whereupon Joan, according to one account, addressed the assembled lords in a loud voice and declared in Christ's name, "I, the Lord Eternal, give France to King Charles!" Commenting on this performance, all of it properly recorded, Pierre Virion says, "Without any argument, devoid of all theoretical considerations, Joan accomplished a clearly political act, showing us politics inseparable from religion, and power without wraps, just as it is, taking its origin from divine authority." In a theological study entitled La Mission de Sainte Jeanne, Fr. Clerissac concluded that:

The proper objective of her mission ... was to remind the world ... that there is a supernatural politics of God, truly at work, dominating the politics of earthly powers, and a Christian body of law which applies and maintains the essential law of this politics, namely the salvation of peoples by means of Christ's Church.

+

The demise of Christendom can be traced without difficulty to the weakness of the French kings. Hardly a century after Joan, Francis I actually sent his ring to Sultan Soliman the Magnificent in a secret gesture of friendship with Islam before the battle of Pavia against the Emperor Charles V. At Lepanto the French were conspicuous by their absence.

On the eve of that decisive battle, Pope St. Pius V would write bitterly to the French monarch regarding:

... this alliance contracted by your illustrious ancestors, which strange illusion and grave error Your Majesty wishes to maintain in the interests of Christianity. This is to forget that one may never do wrong to accomplish good. Your Majesty will not escape reproach if, with a view to personal advantage or any other You may imagine, You persist in preserving friendly relations with infidels ... Your ancestors' offense does not justify your own. God sometimes chastises sons for the faults of their parents. How much more will He exercise His justice on those who presume to perpetuate their fathers' errors!

Under Charles IX similar fatal indulgence was shown to Protestantism, initiating the gradual protestantizing of French politics, which ended by definitively turning France against Spain, and Catholic against Catholic. Under Louis XIV France was not only in the grip of Protestantism and Gallicanism, but even at odds with the Holy See.

It was during his reign that the Sacred Heart appeared on the scene in person at Paray-le-Monial. The Marquis de la Franquerie writes in *Le Sacré Coeur et la France* that our Lord wished:

... to remind the King of the Pact of Tolbiac, the agreement contracted in the Baptistry at Reims, the notarized Act of June 21, 1429 inspired by the Maid of Orleans, in a word, the providential mission of France and her King. Doesn't He have special rights over him? Isn't He addressing the successor of Clovis, Charlemagne, St. Louis, Charles VII, Louis XIII, in fact the very one who owed Him the light of day through a miracle? (Louis XIV's birth had been the answer to prayer for a royal heir on the part of the entire nation.)

The Sacred Heart's appearance at such a time, with demands so political, is clear evidence that He regarded France's former alliances with heaven still very much in force. Furthermore, the extent and nature of the disasters which overtook the whole world after France disregarded these demands testify to the key position she occupies in Christendom. According to the Marquis, "The Church and France remained bereft of the protective shield which Providence wished to give them. After that the reign of the Sacred Heart could establish itself only slowly, progressively, we might say, humanly, in other words in the midst of conflict, trials and the suffering of men left to themselves. Then the 'invisible' enemies of the Church and of France, the Occult Power, secret societies and Freemasonry, as well as the Protestant forces, unleashed their luciferian attacks."

All those in any way responsible for our Lord's rejection suffered punishment. The Society of Jesus, the special instrument chosen by God to propagate devotion to the Sacred Heart, suffered total suppression by order of Clement XIV in 1773. Although it was reconstituted in 1814, it deteriorated spiritually to the point at which we see it today. As for Louis XIV, he was soon forced to abandon the Catholic cause of James II of England and the other Catholic monarchs.

The culmination of the punishment meted out to France and the whole world occurred one hundred years later, to the very day, of the transmission of the message of the Sacred Heart: On June 17, 1789 was constituted the National Assembly which would strip the French monarchy, in the person of Louis XVI, of all power. Four years later he was guillotined. The nation became guilty of sacrilegious regicide.

From that time forth the satanic forces found their way into the heart of the Church much more easily. Shorn of her major temporal protection, she was subjected to the rawest indignity at the hands of the Emperor Joseph and Napoleon. Eventually deprived of her temporal estates, she entered the long succession of humiliations which are now reaching paroxysm.

+

These developments, nonetheless, have never deterred Our Lord from His purpose, which He continued to make known to chosen souls. June 23, 1823 the Sacred Heart declared to Sr. Marie of Jesus in the Convent of les Oiseaux:

> *France is ever dear to my divine Heart, and she shall be consecrated to It. But it must be the King himself who consecrates his family and the whole kingdom ... I am preparing a deluge of grace for France when she is consecrated ... and the whole earth shall feel the blessings I shall pour out on her.*

When Louis XVIII, Louis XVI's younger brother, was put on the throne in 1814, it was only to promulgate a liberal constitution, freedom of the press and religious liberty. He was never properly anointed with the traditional chrism, and in any case showed no inclination to make the consecration of the nation. In 1830 the Blessed Virgin announced to St. Catherine Labouré the fall of his successor Charles X, and told her that it was Jesus Christ himself who would be despoiled in the person of His lieutenant the French king.

France hit a new low after Charles abdicated and was succeeded by Louis Philippe of Orléans, the liberal "bourgeois king," son of the royal traitor Philippe Egalite who had cast the deciding vote for Louis XVI's execution. Louis Philippe was regarded as a usurper by many good Catholics, for according to French law no criminal may inherit anything from his victim, and especially not a kingdom. The Blessed Virgin had also foretold "Satan's triumph forty years later," to Catherine Labouré, and indeed it is recorded that on the evening of September 4, 1870, a huge number of devils brought the news to the demoniac Helene

Poirier that the Third French Republic had just been set up. According to Fr. Champeaux's *Une Possédée Contemporaine*:

> *To manifest their glee, they began singing, laughing and dancing madly. What delighted them, they said, was that their own were at the head of the government, and thus they, the devils, could more easily bring the reign of Jesus Christ to nought.*

Still the Sacred Heart did not abandon His chosen nation. In 1873, through His confidante Madame Royer, He made overtures to the Duke de Chambord, legitimate heir to the throne and fervent devotee of the Sacred Heart, of whom Pius IX had said, "Whatever he says is well said; whatever he does is well done." The Duke forthwith sent a promise in writing to the convent at Paray-le-Monial which was enclosed with St. Margaret Mary's remains, to the effect that he would consecrate France and her army within a year should he regain the throne. He refused all compromise with parliamentarism. Alas, the good Duke was struck by a mortal illness. He was cured miraculously by St. John Bosco, but was warned by him to "beware of the Freemasons." A short time later the Duke fell ill again and died under mysterious circumstances. The anticipated restoration of Christ's kingship never took place.

Throughout these vicissitudes, devotion to the Sacred Heart of Jesus continued to be preached, particularly by well disposed Jesuits. The dissolution of their Order had actually helped their purpose by freeing them for individual action and allowing them to propagate the devotion throughout Europe. It was soon securely established, but mainly as a private devotion. Many Confraternities and Orders dedicated to the Sacred Heart were founded, but despite petitions from the highest quarters, Rome steadfastly refused to authorize a universal Mass and Office of the Sacred Heart until 1856, when Pius IX accorded it the rank of double major. Only in 1889 was it raised to first class rank. In response to directives which our Lord gave to the Good Shepherd nun Bl. Marie of the Divine Heart, the former Maria Droste-zu-Vischering, Leo XIII consecrated the entire human race to the Sacred Heart in 1899. He considered this decree, *Annum Sacrum,* the greatest act of his pontificate.

Following the disorders of the War of 1870, the French Assembly had authorized the construction of the long awaited national Basilica to the Sacred Heart on Montmartre in Paris. Beyond this the devotion received no impetus from the civil government. When the First World War broke out, however, there was a tremendous popular resurgence of devotion. Churches overflowed. Millions of little tricolor pennants with the emblem of the Sacred Heart appeared all over the country, and on the battlefields soldiers affixed them to their rifles and dugouts. They wore the emblem on their uniforms. In June 1915 the French bishops consecrated France to the Sacred Heart, who did not abandon her in her peril.

To the Monarchy He had sent St. Margaret Mary, to the Empire, Mme. Royer. In 1917, when defeat seemed certain for the Allies He would send to the Republic the twenty-year-old Claire Ferchaud, who would found a community vowed to reparation to the Sacred Heart. Her nuns enjoyed the favor of Benedict XV, Cardinal Merry del Val, Pius XII, and even received a blessing from Paul VI. Like a second Joan of Arc Mother Claire promised unconditional victory to the President of the French Republic, Raymond Poincaré, if the Sacred Heart were officially displayed on the white center section of the national tricolor. Reminding him of the promises made to St. Margaret Mary, she relayed the following message from our Lord in a letter dated January 17, 1917:

> *Tell the head of the French government to betake himself to the Basilica of the Sacred Heart of Montmartre with the kings of the allied nations. There the flags of each nation shall be solemnly blessed, whereupon the President must pin the image of My Sacred Heart to each of the standards there present. Then M. Poincaré and all the allied kings at the head of their countries shall officially order the Sacred Heart to be painted on all the flags of every French and Allied regiment. [Apparently the American Utopia would not have been excluded!] All soldiers must be vested with this sign of salvation.*

In March Mother Claire met with the President, who, like Charles VII, had been persuaded of the messenger's authenticity by her knowledge of intimate details of his spiritual life. He promised to lay the matter before the Chamber of Deputies, but at the last moment gave way under pressure from the Freemason Clemenceau's anti-Christian lobby. On May 1 she wrote again, conveying in another message from our Lord:

> *France is putting Me to death but woe to those who will not be converted. The people of France are on the brink of destruction. The traitor lives in France's very heart. It is Freemasonry, which, in order to accomplish the eternal loss of this country, has in conjunction with Germany created this war ... Without Me France would be lost. Freemasonry will be defeated, terrible chastisements will fall on it.*
>
> *But I ask France's brave little soldier, as well as the generals of the armies, to deploy the banner of the Sacred Heart, despite the formal interdiction they will face. Let the generals, officers and simple soldiers move forward! I promise them victory! The Masonic sect, the present government, will be punished. All their traps will be uncovered. Some will be put to death.*

She wrote the generals of the High Command :

> *It is in obedience to God that I have the honor of making His will known to all the Generals of France. Our Lord, who so loves the Franks, is asking them to make an act of faith in His Divine Royalty and to petition the Chief of State to allow the image of the Sacred Heart, sign of hope and salvation, to blaze officially on our national colors.*

Concerted pressure from the military, the clergy, the aristocracy and the bulk of the common people to bring the government around, netted them an order from the Minister of Defense. Dated August 6, 1917, it forbade any such manifestation of piety as a "flagrant violation of liberty of conscience ... and the religious neutrality of the French state." It was even countersigned by General Petain, and the Archbishop of Paris Cardinal Amette urged the faithful to comply.

Nonetheless, Marshal Foch, Commander-in-Chief of the Allied forces, had the courage to disregard the order and consecrated all the armies to the Sacred Heart in the Church of Bombon during the

Octave of the Sacred Heart. This was July 9, 1918, before the second battle of the Marne, when all seemed lost. After asking the local clergy to round up all the children they could find to help him pray, the Marshal began a novena, and on July 18 victory was assured.

The officers and men who had followed Foch's Christian example were rewarded by numerous graces and miracles on the battlefield, and obtained a mitigation of the threatened disaster. The Armistice suspended hostilities, but because Our Lord's conditions were not fully met, the Allies lost the peace. The infamous Treaty of Versailles paved the way for World War II. By this time Our Lady had appeared at Fatima, and Russia had fallen to the Revolution whose errors would infect the whole world. The League of Nations was chartered, and what little was left of Christendom continued to disintegrate before the steady advance of the *gauleiters* of Utopia.

Claire Ferchaud had the gift of miracles. On one occasion in her convent in 1940 she multiplied bread and butter for a band of starving soldiers in retreat who had not eaten for four days. All her life she had been severely molested by the devil. Well aware of the baneful effects of democracy, she wrote in her *Notes Autobiographiques*, "Whoever occupies a place of preeminence can only produce ruin if he is not chosen by God." She referred to Freemasonry as "the weapon of Satan, the brain of Lucifer, the inspirer of the atheist Republic," and maintained that modern wars were "waged by the magnetic breath of man spiritualized not by God, but by infernal forces."

She ascribed the disorganization of French society to its regicide: "France is only a decapitated body, she bears the punishment of her fault in her descendants, who cannot live without rejoining its members to the head of a Monarch and finding again in his veins the blood of a Sovereign." She predicted that with "France gone, her soul stifled, the Church will be only a tottering ruin which will fall in its turn."

In 1959 she wrote, "Something like the fall of Lucifer is being repeated in our France," and that if the desires of the Sacred Heart had been met, "The last forty years would not have been flooded by the overflow of bloodshed in continual warfare." Until her death in 1972 she maintained that despite peace treaties, hostilities had never ceased, and that "the wars will continue." The Sacred Heart had told her that there could be no lasting peace until His Vicar was invited to the conference table. He appeared to her with a huge gash in His Sacred Heart, caused by France, yet He promised her, "Oh, how beautiful France will be one day! No, try as Satan will, France will never be his!"

At the outset of World War II Marshal Pétain was asked, as head of the legitimate French government in Vichy, to make the long desired Consecration. In only one instance has a modern republic been consecrated to the Sacred Heart of Jesus. This was done by Garcia Moreno when he assumed the Presidency of Ecuador. Unfortunately the Christian regime he inaugurated and the reforms he instituted were brought to an end by his assassination in 1875. Marshal Pétain would have been happy to do likewise, but felt he could not do so in the case of France.

Although he agreed fervently in principle, he was constrained to acknowledge, "Where the Consecration of France to the Sacred Heart is concerned, only the King of France is qualified to make it, in order to give it full force ... I am only the Chief of State, I am not the King." St. John the Baptist couldn't have put it better. With the fall of the legal Vichy government, General de Gaulle established the present Republic. Its Constitution, like that of its inspiration the American Utopia, formally repudiates France's divine mission under God by affirming secularity on principle. Under the growing utopian tyranny, Sacred Heart devotion was soon divested of all political significance.

Since the Council, it has been downgraded even as a means of personal sanctification. As Claire Ferchaud predicted, the Church herself, abandoned by the Christian rulers God had appointed to protect her, is beginning to share their fate. As reported in *The Centre-Réform Catholique* for July 1990, the American Archbishop John May inadvertently acknowledged this when he remarked:

> *Catholic doctrine and moral teaching are largely judged according to the criteria of the democratic spirit and practice. Hence the very fact of stating that there is an authoritative Church teaching that binds and looses for all eternity is certainly a sign of contradiction for many Americans who regard the divine right of bishops as outmoded as the divine right of kings.*

In the heat of the destruction, Jacques Maritain, mentor of Paul VI, continued to be charmed by American pluralism. He rejoiced to see how the Church:

> *...renouncing the protection of the secular sword, emancipates herself from the bothersome guardianship of the Catholic heads of state, and contenting herself with liberty alone, reduces herself now to being no more than the evangelical yeast hidden in the dough as the sign of salvation for humanity.*

Could there be more formal denial of the Kingship of Christ?

In *Le Caractère Sacré et Divin de la Royauté en France*, the Marquis de la Franquerie calls the Church's present situation the result of:

> *... the introduction of democracy into her bosom and the agents of hell into her leadership ... The message of Paray-le-Monial numbers relentless adversaries in all places and among all parties ... That is because it would lead, were our Lord's requests properly met, to the establishment of the Kingship of Christ over France in particular and through her, over the whole world. Now, Satan-Lucifer does not want this rule, so puts everything in motion to discredit the Message. His natural allies are judeo-masonry, liberalism, modernism, progressism and all the supporters of the democratism which is more or less in fief to the Lodges and blinded by ignorant anti-clericalism.*

In 1925, in the teeth of all this, Pope Pius XI canonically established the feast of Christ the King with the encyclical *Quas primas*, which voiced once more the message of the Sacred Heart to the effect that, "not only individuals, but also rulers and princes are bound to give public honor and obedience to Christ," and it made clear that "the title and power of King belongs to Christ as man in the strict and proper sense," and not just "figuratively and spiritually." Hamish Fraser called this pronouncement "the greatest non-event in the entire history of the Church ... all but completely ignored, especially by the so-called Catholic nations and by the Catholic clergy."

The unprecedented evils now engulfing the world are the direct result of the stubborn refusal on the part of Kings and Presidents to consecrate temporal authority to the Sacred Heart in accordance with the order reigning in Heaven. Incredible as it may seem, today we are witnessing a similar unwillingness on the part of Pontiffs and Bishops from Pius XI on down to accede to another merciful intervention from Heaven requesting the consecration of Russia to the Immaculate Heart of Mary.

In 1931, never tiring in patience, the Sacred Heart appeared to Sr. Lucy, the *portavoz* of Fatima, and He referred ominously to the King of France. Reporting the communication to her Bishop, Sr. Lucy says our Lord told her, "Make it known to my ministers that if they follow the example of the King of France in delaying the execution of My request, that they will follow him into misfortune." In another account written five years later she writes, "Our Lord complainingly said to me, 'They did not want to heed my request. Like the King of France they will repent and do so, but it will be late. Russia will already have spread her errors throughout the world, causing wars and persecutions of the Church. The Holy Father will have much to suffer!'"

In a letter dated May 26,1846, three years before the fateful "year of revolutions" struck Europe, Juan Donoso Cortes summed it all up to his liberal pen pal, the Duke de Montalembert:

> *There is no period of history which doesn't end in catastrophe. The first period of history began with creation and ended in the Flood. And what does the Flood signify? Two things: the natural triumph of evil over good and the supernatural triumph of God over evil, by means of a direct, personal, sovereign act.*
>
> *Men were still wringing wet with the waters of the Flood, when the same battle started up again ... At our Lord's coming it was everywhere night, deep, palpable night. The Lord is raised on the cross, and daylight returns to the world. What does that great catastrophe signify? Two things: the natural triumph of evil over good, and the supernatural triumph of God over evil, by means of a direct, personal, sovereign act.*
>
> *What does Scripture say of the end of the world? It says that the Antichrist will be lord of the universe, and that the last judgment will take place at that time, along with the last*

catastrophe. Like the others, it will signify the natural triumph of evil over good, and the supernatural triumph of God over evil, by means of a direct, personal, sovereign act.

And don't tell me that if defeat is certain, fighting is useless. In the first place, fighting can lessen, can soften the catastrophe; and in the second place, for us whose glory it is to be Catholic, fighting is the accomplishment of a duty, not the result of calculation. Let's thank God for having allowed us to do battle. Beyond this favor, let's not seek the grace to win. For those who fight generously for His cause, His infinite goodness reserves a reward far greater and more precious to man than victory here below.

Devotion to the Sacred Heart of Jesus tells us what we really mean when we pray in the Lord's Prayer, "Thy kingdom come!" The magnitude of the disaster facing us is not only the measure, but the harbinger of the final triumph. The message delivered at Paray-le-Monial is not mere private revelation which may be bypassed without danger to salvation. It relates directly to the deposit of faith and can be found throughout Scripture.

Before His Ascension into heaven our Lord charged His disciples to "teach all nations," and not just individuals (*Matt.28:19*). And again in the Apocalypse, when the seventh angel sounds the trumpet, "great voices in heaven" are heard saying, "The Kingdom of this world is become our Lord's and His Christ's, and He shall reign forever and ever!" (*Apo. 11:15*). And we still have our Lord's promise to St. Margaret Mary that "I will reign in spite of Satan and all opposition!"

Sooner or later, Christ the King will deal with Utopia.

LOUIS XVI:
PROTOMARTYR OF UTOPIA

Without counting the millions of its aborted children, Utopia has produced untold numbers of martyrs, and no doubt heaven will be peopled by many more before the battle is over. The vast majority are unknown, but in a work dealing with the utopian desolation, it would be unseemly not to mention at least one of them. This chapter will therefore tell something of King Louis XVI of France. As King of the kings of Christendom, he can be said to be their official representative, recapitulating them all in his person as temporal head of Christ's kingdom on earth. Not in the order of time, but in the order of dignity, he is, as it were, the Protomartyr of Utopia.

Ascertaining the facts of his life is not as easy as might be supposed, for much has been suppressed, and more has been distorted. During the French Revolution a motion was laid before the Conventional Assembly to make public a record which had been kept of the daily doings of King Louis during his incarceration prior to his execution. It was vehemently opposed by Hébert, Procurator of the Commune, who warned the delegates:

It would be bad policy, indeed dangerous, to put before the eyes of the people a relation revealing the kind of fortitude Louis displayed on the scaffold. Do you want to excite pity for the tyrant's fate in the people? His head has fallen, we must concern ourselves only with recounting his misdeeds. In short, history must be written for the people; this history must portray Louis in eradicable terms, as ordering citizens massacred on August 10, as forming a coalition with all the European monarchs to destroy the sacred edifice of freedom ... But the private life of this despot must be buried in the most profound oblivion. Ah, beware, Citizens, lest the people shake off the feelings of hatred for kings which they must retain forever, feelings which you must endeavor to kindle and sustain.

Two hundred years later, as the democratic experiment severs its last ties with created reality, there are signs that the manufactured hatred for kings is indeed wearing thin among the people. Pointing out what a fiasco the 1989 government-sponsored Bicentenary of the French Revolution had turned out to be, the *Monarchist League Newsletter* declared, "Active French monarchists are still relatively few. However ... slowly things are beginning to change, with those who once laughed at the idea of a restoration in France now having to take the matter much more seriously."

With the close of the Quincentenary of the discovery of America, rife with fresh denigrations of Columbus, Queen Isabella and Pope Alexander VI, 1993 opened on January 21 with a bicentennial commemoration of the execution of His Most Christian Majesty Louis XVI, by the grace of God King of France and Navarre. Plans had been laid in November 1990, when the *"Association pour le Bicentennaire de la Mort de Louis XVI"* was formed to encourage study of his life and martyrdom among historians and the general public. The group does not regard itself as a political movement, but hopes to be instrumental in restoring proper perspective on one of the noblest heroes of Christendom.

From the scaffold King Louis absolved the French people as a whole of any responsibility for the regicide, which he knew to be the work of a powerful Jacobin minority. Those acquainted with the facts maintain that, had not the occult forces laboring to destroy the Faith not succeeded in eliminating him, his reign would have been one of unprecedented glory and prosperity.

What schoolchildren have been taught about Louis XVI for the past two hundred years is very different. Here is a fair sample, taken from a 1958 edition of the popular American World Book Encyclopedia:

> *Louis XVI (1754-1793), the grandson of Louis XV, came to the throne in 1774. He was a man of personal virtue and good intentions, but was a weak ruler. He was more interested in hunting than in public affairs. In 1770, he married the beautiful Marie Antoinette of Austria. Louis often relied on the advice of his wife. But she was unpopular because of her frivolity and her extravagance, etc., etc.*

Not mentioned is the fact that in the exuberance of his youth this same king had resolved "to etch the precepts of Religion deep in my soul, and when I pray to God, the acts of adoration I render to Him exteriorly shall be preceded by the homage of my heart." With all the overconfidence of tender inexperience he had promised, "I shall be recollected, full of faith, love and fervor!" These were not idle words, however, for he had been formed in piety from earliest infancy by parents and preceptors beyond the ordinary.

His mother, Marie-Josephe of Saxony, had promised on the feast of the Presentation of Our Lady to rear all her children for God, and both she and her husband have since been proposed as candidates for beatification. Three of their children likewise may well be raised to the honors of the altar: Clothilde, Queen of Sardinia, has already been declared Venerable; a process has been opened for her sister Elizabeth, whom Pope Pius VII regarded as a saint; and as we shall see, their brother Louis is probably even better qualified, for his would be the martyr's palm.

Wrote he:

All my life I purpose, to be simply and generously Christian, without affectation or singularity, rising all the while above every kind of human respect. I make a firm and sincere resolution to be highly, publicly and generously faithful to Him who holds all kings and kingdoms in His hand. I can be great only in Him, because in Him alone resides greatness and glory, majesty and strength; and I am destined one day to be His living image on earth.

Little did he realize then how closely he would be called to conform to the heavenly model. Little did he foresee that he would become the "living image" of the divine King not so much by governing his people, as had his sainted ancestor St. Louis IX before him, as by suffering and dying for them. Most dramatically he would set before the world not the Rule, but the Passion of Christ the King.

Such was the destiny of this young prince, who understood so clearly that every monarch exercising dominion over his subjects is but the reflection of Christ the King, whose Father is Creator and Ruler of all things visible and invisible. Put to death by those to whom he was sent to govern, he would portray for them the Royal Victim rejected and betrayed by His subjects, who yet lay down His life for them. Like Him, here below Louis would rule not from the throne, but from the Cross. His subjects would be asked by a usurping authority, "Shall I crucify your king?" (*John 19:15*), and they too would be misled, in the name of democracy, to vote in the affirmative.

"Religion should be the only politics of kings," Louis had proclaimed:

> *Where there is Religion, no other politics is necessary. I shall not rule according to inclination, but according to duty', and I shall insist that the Catholic, Apostolic, and Roman Religion continue to be the religion of the state ... To know God and make Him known, such is my wish. These two words comprise all the craft of government.*

Such were the sentiments of the last real king of France, and they cost him his life. This virtuous king, represented to the public as "more interested in hunting than in public affairs," inevitably drew the implacable hatred of the satanic forces arrayed against Christ himself.

Like Christopher Columbus, Philip II, Mary Queen of Scots and other servants of God in high places, Louis became even in his lifetime the target of the calculated calumny which is hell's last recourse against the upright. His alleged irresponsibility, weak intellect and ineptitude in money matters became accepted without question even by those well disposed towards him, along with Philip of Spain's sadism and torture chambers, Columbus' extramarital love and the Scottish Queen's aberrations - accusations no more supported by proof than the current fiction of man's evolution from animal life.

Historians must dig deep to ferret out the truth today, for the campaign of perversion and suppression of facts has formed a heavy crust in history texts and Hollywood-inspired fiction alike. After two centuries of indoctrination, only a few intrepid souls in France like Girault de Coursac or the Marquis de la Franquerie, on whom we draw heavily, have the discernment to speak truly. It was not easy to defame Louis, however, for his gentle affability and goodness were known to all who had any contact with him, as countless memoirs of the period reveal.

His enemies therefore labored to make him out a ninny. His weakness of intellect - a palpable falsehood quickly dispelled by reading almost anything he wrote - was immediately put into circulation by international Masonry's apostolate to the uninformed in every court in Europe. Prince Henry of Prussia, brother of Frederick the Great, was only one of many thus misled. After a meeting with Louis, however, he wrote a French acquaintance:

> *What surprised me most was your King. I had formed a completely different idea of him. I was astonished to discover on talking with him that he was so well educated, that he held such exact notions of politics, that the well-being of his people absorbed him entirely, and that he was replete with common sense!*

Other tactics were used against his beautiful Queen, whose outspoken simplicity and love of fun made her an easy mark. Although her modesty and virtue were exemplary, she was reported to be unfaithful to her husband. This particular slander was especially promoted by those would-be seducers of the court whom she had mortally antagonized by indignantly rejecting their improper advances. (One, alas, was a Cardinal of the Church and woefully influential.)

The truth is that her modesty was such that she shrank even from having her hair dressed in the presence of others as protocol then demanded, and as to her supposed frivolity and love of finery, it is of record that before Louis' accession to the throne the old King's aunts repeatedly reprimanded her for her simple attire, which they considered unbefitting a future queen and prejudicial to French manufacturers. "My state and court attire," she replied on one occasion, "shall not be less brilliant than those of any former Dauphiness or Queen of France, if such be the pleasure of the King, but to my grandfather-in-law Louis XV I appeal for some indulgence with respect to my private costume in the mornings." This was recorded by her equally virtuous friend and attendant the Princess de Lamballe, who also relates, "So much did she delight in being unshackled by finery that she would hurry from Court to fling off her royal robes and ornaments, exclaiming when free of them, 'Thank heaven, I'm out of harness!'" As for her supposedly lavish expenditures, Lamballe tells us:

Her allowance as Queen of France was no more than 300,000 francs. It is well known that she was generous, liberal and very charitable, that she paid all her expenses regularly respecting her household, Trianon, her dresses, diamonds, millinery and everything else - her Court establishment excepted, and some few items paid by the civil list. She was one of the foremost queens of Europe, had the first establishment in Europe and was obliged to maintain the most refined and luxurious in Europe, and all upon means no greater than had been assigned to many former bigoted queens who led cloistered lives retired from the world without circulating their wealth among the nation which supplied them with so large a revenue ... Such was the goodness of heart of the excellent Queen of Louis XVI, such the benevolence of her character, that not only did she support all the pensioners left by her predecessors, but she distributed through public and private charities sums greater than any of the former Queens, thus increasing her expenses without any proportionate augmentation of her resources.

The young queen also instituted such minor reforms as lay within her power:

The decorum of Marie Antoinette would not allow her to endure those public exhibitions of the ceremony of dressing herself which had been customary at Court. This reserve was highly approved by His Majesty, and one of the first reforms she introduced after the accession was in the internal discipline of her apartment.

Her very rectitude proved her undoing. The Princess, who remained faithful to her to the last and was brutally knifed to death in prison, tells us:

Never should I have been so firmly and so long attached to Marie Antoinette, had I not known that her thorough native goodness of heart had been warped and misguided - though acting at the same time with the best intentions - by a false notion that her genuine innocence would prove a sufficient shield against public censure of such innovations upon national prejudices as she thought proper to introduce.

It was characteristic of Marie Antoinette that she refused to shed the crocodile tears court etiquette demanded at the funeral of the former King Louis XV. The famous deluge which followed his reign never originated in her eyes, but she incurred much criticism from those who indulged in the required transports of official grief. Her same reliance on her own innocence also explains how she would fall prey so easily to the machinations of the Cardinal de Rohan and his occultist intimate Cagliostro in the famous affair of the diamond necklace, a scandal in which she was in no way implicated, but which was used to degrade her beyond remedy before the public.

In his *Morals and Dogma*, Masonry's Luciferian high priest Albert Pike reveals:

Cagliostro was an agent of the Templars, and therefore wrote to the Freemasons of London that the time had come to begin the work of the rebuilding of the Temple of the Eternal. He had introduced into Masonry a new Rite called the Egyptian, and endeavored to resuscitate the mysterious worship of Isis. The three letters L "P"D" on his seal were the initials of the words Lilia pedibus destrue, *'tread underfoot the Lilies (of France),' and a Masonic medal of the sixteenth or seventeenth century has upon it a sword cutting off the stalk of a lily and the words* talem dabit ultio messem, *'such harvest revenge will give.'*

The adepts of Masonry well knew that the French monarchy was the pivot upon which all Christian society turned. Continues Pike:

A lodge under the auspices of Rousseau, the fanatic of Geneva became the center of the revolutionary movement in France, and a Prince of the blood-royal went thither to swear the destruction of the successors of Philippe le Bel on the tomb of Jacques Molay. The registers of the Order of Templars attest that the Regent, the Duc d'Orléans, was Grand Master of the formidable Secret Society, and that his successors were the Duc de Maine, the Prince of Bourbon-Condé and the Duc de Cossé-Brissac.

Such were the enemies lying in wait for the young King of France, who everyone agreed was good-natured to a fault. The Englishwoman Catherine Hyde, Marquise de Broglie Scolari, who made herself so useful to the French royal family during their captivity, and who edited the Princess de Lamballe's journal from which we have quoted, characterized Louis as "a lamb who had to rule tigers." He forgave enemies so readily and from the heart, especially ecclesiastics, that he could never bring himself to treat them with the severity the situation demanded. The people he considered merely misled, as indeed they were, and begged God's forgiveness for their atrocities who "know not what they do."

+

Sober facts will not support a charge of misgovernment against Louis, whose reign was unusually auspicious in its beginnings. His foes, like those of "good farmer George" III in America, had considerable trouble making him out a tyrant, but as they had defamed the King of kings long ago in Jerusalem, equally adroit agitators and propagandists in Paris "persuaded" and "moved the people" (*Matt. 27:20; Mk. 15:11*) to believe falsehood. Among his first aims was to rid his court of undesirables, a procedure sure to arouse the displeasure of the profligate; yet even here he exercised clemency.

The late King's mistress Madame du Barry, says Lamballe:

> *...was much better dealt with by the young King, whom she had always treated with the greatest levity, than she or her numerous courtiers expected. She was allowed her pension and the entire enjoyment of her ill-gotten accumulated wealth, but of course, excluded from ever appearing at Court, and politically exiled from Paris.*

There may have been other reasons for such leniency, for there is some evidence that Louis XV was married to Mme. du Barry in a secret morganatic marriage, of which his grandson may have been aware. In any case, the royal couple "were looked upon as models of goodness. The virtues of Louis XVI were so generally known that all France hastened to acknowledge them, whereas the Queen's fascinations acted like a charm on all who had not been invincibly prejudiced against the many excellent qualities which entitled her to love and admiration.

> *Indeed, I never heard an insinuation against either the King or the Queen but from those depraved minds which never possessed virtue enough to imitate theirs, or were jealous of the wonderful powers of pleasing that so eminently distinguished Marie Antoinette from the rest of her sex.*

Sad to relate, one such "depraved mind" seems to have been that of the American Ambassador Thomas Jefferson, who as late as 1786 wrote home sardonically, "When our king goes out, they fall down and kiss the earth where he has trodden; and then they go to kissing one another. And this is the truest wisdom."

There was heavy popular support for the first decrees of Louis' administration. Under his leadership the economic situation brightened; agriculture, commerce, arts and sciences flourished. He was eminently successful in rebuilding the French navy, which soon eclipsed the English. Newly built Cherbourg rivaled Portsmouth as a major port, and foreign potentates began sending their officers to France rather than England for training, causing Pitt to declare in the British House of Commons that England could never attain the supremacy of the seas while the Bourbon dynasty endured.

The dark role played behind the scenes by English Judeo-Masonry in bringing down the French monarchy is well known. The Marquis de la Franquerie says of Louis, "No other of our kings had the glory of raising such a manifestation of hatred on the part of France's worst enemies." This explains how in self-defense and for reasons of political expediency he was induced to lay aside his Catholic aversion for revolutionary democracy and throw the might of France on the side of Colonial America, in hopes of weakening England. (To this day Louisville, Kentucky bears his name and sports the lilies of France on its official banner.) He might also have foreseen that, at the price of separation of Church and state, the American Revolution would serve to break the iron grip by which the English heretics throttled the Faith in the Colonies.

For her part, Louis' royal consort considered herself under no social obligations to the American rebels, let alone to lend support to their new order of the ages. Not long before her execution, when her friend the Princess "mentioned to Her Majesty the affectionate sympathy expressed by the King and Queen of England for her sufferings, and their regret at the state of public affairs in France," Marie Antoinette could reply in all honesty:

> *It is most noble and praiseworthy in them to feel thus, and the more so considering the illiberal part imputed to us against those sovereigns in the rebellion of their subjects overseas, to which, heaven knows, I never gave my approbation. Had I done so, how poignant would be my remorse at the retribution of our sufferings, and the pity of those I had so injured!*
>
> *No, I was perhaps the only silent individual among millions of infatuated enthusiasts at General Lafayette's return to Paris, nor did I sanction any of the entertainments given to Dr. Franklin or the American ambassadors at the time. I could not conceive it prudent for the Queen of an absolute monarchy to countenance any of their newfangled philosophical experiments with my presence. Now I feel the reward of my conscience. I exult in my freedom from a self-reproach which would have been utterly insupportable under the kindness of which you speak.*

Although for reasons of state Louis XVI was constrained to receive the American rebel representatives at court, his private opinion of Benjamin Franklin certainly coincided with that of his wife. It is well illustrated by the following anecdote related by Mme. Campan:

> *Even at the palace of Versailles, at the exposition of Sevres porcelains, there was being sold under the eyes of the King a medallion of Franklin bearing the inscription* Eripuit coelo fulmen sceptrumque tyrannis *... As a joke he ordered a chamber pot from the Sevres factory, with the inscription so much in vogue in the bottom of it, and sent it to the Countess Diane de Polignac [very taken with Franklin] for a New Year's present.*

Obviously the Queen was a woman of spirit. We can imagine what kind of press she received in democratic circles after publicly snubbing Benjamin Franklin, already czar of the international revolutionary media operating out of Holland, not to mention the other American emissaries high in the ranks of world Masonry. As for their friend the Marquis de Lafayette, so idolized in revolutionary America, not even King Louis could find any good to say of him: All the while he pretended to serve his King as Commandant of the troops at Versailles, "Popularity and ambition have made him the principal promoter of republicanism. Having failed of becoming a Washington, he is mad to become a Cromwell. I have no faith in these turncoat constitutionalists."

The Princess says the Marquis:

> *... considered nothing paramount to public notoriety. To this he had sacrificed the interests of his country and trampled underfoot the throne, but finding he could not succeed in forming a Republican government in France as he had in America, he like many others lost his popularity with the demagogues ... Her Majesty certainly saw him frequently, but never again would she put herself in the way of being betrayed by one whom she considered faithless to all.*

Utopia has never forgiven Marie Antoinette. Jefferson, who presented his credentials at Versailles in 1785, did not fail to do his bit to discredit her. He wrote in his Autobiography:

> *This angel, as gaudily painted in the rhapsodies of the Rhetor Burke, with some smartness of fancy but no sound sense, was proud, disdainful of restraint, indignant at all obstacles to her will, eager in the pursuit of pleasure and firm enough to hold to her desires or perish in their wreck.*
>
> *Her inordinate gambling and dissipations, with those of the Count of Artois and others of her clique, had been a sensible item in the exhaustion of the treasury, which called into action the reforming hand of the nation; and her opposition to it, her inflexible perseverance and dauntless spirit led herself to the Guillotine and drew the king with her and plunged the world into crimes and calamities which will forever stain the pages of*

*modern history. I have ever believed that had there been no
queen, there would have been no revolution.*

Such words from an intimate of the most powerful Illuminati of
the day reveal clearly the slant which the higher councils had
determined on giving to the new "history for the people." The
fictitious extravagances of a depraved Queen would be given out as
the cause of the temporary financial crisis which was used to
provoke the carefully planned Revolution. Actually, the deficit was
only the natural result of the necessary military buildup and the
heavy loans to America - for which, incidentally, Louis never
demanded either interest or return of capital. The expenditures were
not only fully justified at the time, but by today's standards were
utterly negligible on a per capita basis.

Be it noted in passing that Napoleon's future spectacular rise to
power would rest primarily on the armed forces so admirably
reorganized by Louis, and not by him. Historians like Nesta
Webster have since advanced proof that the crisis itself, like many
another, was artificially exacerbated in order to further the plans of
the conspirators. The corn crops, for instance, were bought up to
cause famine among the people, who at the same time were told that
their Queen had dismissed the plight of the breadless with the
famous fabricated quip, "Let them eat cake!"

Compassion for his subjects had in fact led Louis to declare,
"Let us be misers of the public treasury. Often it is the price of the
sweat, and sometimes the tears of the people." On the occasion of
his daughter's First Holy Communion, when French princesses
traditionally received a diamond necklace, the royal parent decided
to eliminate so costly a gift. "I know you are too reasonable, my
daughter," he told her:

> *... to think that you would attach any great value to
> artificial finery at a time when you must be entirely concerned
> with decking your heart and making it a sanctuary worthy of
> the Divinity. Besides, my child, public misery is so extreme, the
> poor so numerous, surely you would rather do without gems
> than know they lack bread ... Daughter, pray for France and for
> Us. The prayers of the innocent can turn aside heaven's wrath.*

How well this enlightened King understood that:

> *Sovereigns were given to the people, and not the people to sovereigns. Supreme authority is merely the right to govern, and to govern is not to enjoy, but to give joy to others ... A sovereign's liberty is no different from that of his people: He is not permitted to will all he can; like them he is obliged to will only what he ought.*

Regarding the unlimited freedom of the press being promoted by the Revolution, he wrote his minister Malesherbes:

> *I love and appreciate men who prove by useful books that they make good use of their lights, but I will never encourage by any special benefit productions which tend to general demoralization. Keep a close watch to see that bad books receive as little publicity as possible. License must be bridled, for without such means Religion and morals would soon lose strength. Our modern philosophers have exalted the benefits of freedom only that they might with greater audacity cast seeds of rebellion into hearts. You have issued orders in my name to prosecute impious books. We shall keep our word.*

As the Marquis de la Franquerie notes:

> *For any impartial observer the reign of Louis XVI, had it not been terminated by the French Revolution, would have been one of the best and most glorious for France. Besides, history shows not only that France never wanted the Revolution - this last having been unleashed by an impious conspiracy in the pay of Judeo-Masonic-Protestant powers who were the worst enemies of France and Christendom - but that the King was unable and could not have been able to avoid it, the secret societies having infiltrated and immobilized all the wheels of government.*

Three years before the Revolution erupted, the death of Louis had already been decided on by Freemasons in session in Frankfurt, Germany.

His fate was sealed, however, not because Masonry decreed it, but because his sacrifice had been accepted on high. Like his Lord and Model in Kingship, Louis would be led like a lamb to the slaughter, as an offering on behalf of the people. The principle for which he lay down his life was clear. In *Louis XVI et sa Béatification*, Mgr. Delassus says of him:

> *He believed that the dogma of the sovereignty of the people, which was beginning to be professed, was the impudent negation of the rights of God over society and of the right given to His Church to teach and direct kings and peoples in the paths of salvation. He used to say that the essence of authority was not to be an intermediary, but to be in charge.*

Pressed by the Assembly to sidestep this duty by approving a civil Constitution for the French clergy, Louis wrote in desperation to the Pope:

> *It would render them independent of the Holy See; it would allow their election by the people; it would overthrow the age-old hierarchy of the Church, and in order to gain adherents for this civil Constitution of the Clergy and to expel the faithful priests, they want to exact an oath. Most Holy Father, this oath will cause a schism in the Church! A nameless dread pierces me with fear. I see Religion vilified, its ministers persecuted, the wolf in the sheepfold. I wanted You to be the first to know of this resolution of the Estates-General, the project of a few hotheads, of some persons deeply perverted and already highly skilled in the art of revolution.*

What Louis saw was democracy usurping the powers of the Church as it had those of the state. In panic he begs the Pope for help: "I need Your advice and shall do nothing without consulting You. I shall send You a copy of this Constitution. Examine it. Your wise counsel will guide me. But already the voice of my conscience cries out that I must not sanction this work of darkness." Of this man Jefferson had the effrontery to write, "The king goes for nothing. He hunts one half of the day, is drunk the other, and signs whatever he is bid." And on another occasion, "His mind was weakness itself, his constitution timid, his judgment null, and without sufficient firmness even to stand by the faith of his word."

Pope Pius VI forthwith delegated two French Archbishops to advise the King and to oppose the measure before the Assembly by all possible means, but unfortunately, in the vain hope of averting worse disaster, these prelates ended by persuading Louis to grant his approval against his conscience. As he foresaw, there ensued a savage persecution of the faithful clergy who refused the required oath. One of the Archbishops died of grief and remorse; the other recanted publicly. The Civil Constitution for the Clergy was formally condemned by Papal Brief dated April 8, 1790.

The King, although not held responsible by the Pope or anyone else, saw fit in the beautiful last testament he wrote on Christmas Day, 1792, to beg God's forgiveness "for having put my name (although this was against my will) to acts which could be contrary to the discipline and belief of the Church." Despite this misstep, all the while making every concession compatible with the Faith, Louis never formally entertained the democratic heresy which has since destroyed Christendom and is now engulfing the whole world in utopian madness. At best, for him it had been a lesser evil forced upon him by circumstances.

To his brothers, who by then were residing outside France, he wrote:

> *You have no doubt been informed that I have accepted the Constitution, and you know the reasons I gave to the Assembly, but these must not suffice for you. I wish to make known to you all my motives. The state of France is such that she is on the verge of complete dissolution, which will only be hastened if violent remedies are brought to bear on all the ills which are overwhelming her.*
>
> *The party spirit that divides her, and the destruction of all authority are the causes of all her trouble. Divisions must be made to cease and authority reestablished, but for this purpose only two means are possible: union or force. Force can only be employed by foreign armies, and this means having recourse to war. Can a King allow himself to carry war into his own states? Is not the remedy worse than the disease?*

The good-natured Louis was convinced that in due time "public opinion would change." It did not change, for the people of France never wanted democracy in the first place. They were as much victims of the conspiracy as was their monarch. On January 21, 1793, when the head of Louis Capet was severed from his body by the guillotine, not only was the French nation by the selfsame stroke severed from its anointed ruler, but all Christendom lost its head, because it is upon the French king, King of the kings of Christendom, that Christ was pleased to rest his Kingship in the temporal order.

Having consummated their own Revolution a generation before that of France, the English in America must be credited with having provided the preamble to this mortal blow to Christendom. Cardinal Pie called France henceforth a body without a head, adding dryly, "Well, a headless body, no matter how well organized you may think it, is nothing but a corpse," a conclusion applying to democracies and artificial nations generally. Commenting on the catastrophe at the time, Joseph de Maistre had this to say:

> *Undoubtedly one of the greatest crimes it is possible to commit is assault upon sovereignty, no other having such terrible consequences. If sovereignty resides in one head, and this head falls victim to the assault, the atrocity of the crime is increased. But if this sovereign has deserved his fate through no crime, if his very virtues have armed the guilty against him, the crime is beyond naming.*
>
> *By such marks we recognize the death of Louis XVI; but the most important thing to note is that no crime ever had more accomplices ... Each drop of Louis XVI's blood will cost France torrents; four million French will pay with their heads for the great national crime of an anti-religious, anti-social insurrection crowned by regicide.*

After two major world wars and countless lesser conflicts hatched by utopian democracy, de Maistre's estimate seems modest indeed.

With the fall of France the other Christian monarchies toppled one by one as expected, reaching a climax with that of the Holy Roman Emperor Karl of Hapsburg at the close of the first of the world wars. There remains only one serious obstacle to the complete triumph of Satan, which Albert Pike has kindly pointed out for the duller-witted among us: "The secret movers of the French Revolution had sworn to overturn the Throne and the Altar upon the Tomb of Jacques de Molay. When Louis XVI was executed, half the work was done; and thenceforward the Army of the Temple was to direct all its efforts against the Pope." This maneuver is still in progress.

+

Knowing he would not be allowed to address his people from the scaffold, Louis XVI proclaimed his innocence in the only way left to him, as Charles I of England had done: He wore white. "I die innocent of all the crimes imputed to me," he began, "I forgive the perpetrators of my death, and I pray God that the blood you are about to shed never falls on France," but a roll of drums drowned out his voice. His last words were, "I render my soul to God." Whereupon the faithful Fr. Edgeworth de Firmont, a refuser of the clerical oath who attended His Majesty in his last hours, is credited with declaring solemnly as the knife fell, "Son of St. Louis, ascend to heaven!"

No one was more aware of the religious dimensions of the sacrifice just consummated on the Place de la Concorde than the regicides themselves. The revolutionary journalist Prudhomme reported:

> *A citizen climbed onto the guillotine, and plunging his naked arm into the blood of Louis Capet which was gushing copiously, took handfuls and three times sprinkled the crowd of spectators, who were pressing the foot of the scaffold to receive a drop on their foreheads. 'Brothers,' said the citizen as he performed his* asperges, *'we have been threatened with the blood of Louis Capet falling on our heads. Well, then, let it fall!'*

We are infallibly reminded of those who shouted against Christ their King in Pilate's court, "His blood be upon us and upon our children!" (*Matt. 27:25*). A black Mass was celebrated that night with the King's blood on the outskirts of Paris.

Was Louis XVI a martyr in the canonical sense? Like those who put the Son of God to death, his murderers were the first to suspect and fear this was indeed the case. As with our Lord, who had been accused of stirring up the people to make himself king, every effort was made to give the accusations against Louis a purely political cast, treating him as an enemy of the people, one who insisted on favoring only those clergy and laity who opposed the glorious aims of the Revolution.

The deliberations of the Assembly, however, revealed the true cause of his death sentence: Records show that one of the members moved that a letter written by the King to the Bishop of Clermont expressing the royal desire to re-establish Catholic worship as soon as possible, be entered as evidence by the prosecution. When the letter was read aloud from the floor, a certain Serre protested, "that worship not be mentioned, unless you want to see him one day canonized!" It was therefore decided to level against the royal defendant only the charge that, "The nation accuses you of having manifested the will and desire of recovering your former power."

According to M. de Coursac, it was the aforementioned Jacobin editor Prudhomme who first took cognizance in print that:

> *Priests and devout ladies already searching their calendars for a place for Louis XVI among the martyrs, have noted parallels between his execution and the passion of their Christ. Following the example of the Jewish people of Jerusalem, the people of Paris tore Louis Capet's frock-coat in two -* scinderunt vestimenta mea - *each desiring to take home a scrap.*

It is true that shortly after the execution, a friend of the King's saintly sister Madame Elisabeth, Fr. de Lubersac, wrote a little work on the "passion of Louis" comparing it to our Lord's, entitled *Rapprochement et Paralléle des Souffrances de Jésus-Christ avec celles de Louis XVI*. The theme was revived in 1902 by Armand Cranel, a lawyer from Toulouse who presented to Pope Leo XIII a volume called *The Real Louis XVI*, which was released to the public in 1913. It remained for Girault de Coursac in 1950, and again in 1976, to juxtapose the pertinent scriptural texts of the Passion with quotations from firsthand historical sources not previously available. His *Louis XVI Roi Martyr?* makes a powerful little document.

For instance, he finds our Lord's lament over Jerusalem in these words of Louis: "I see the people delivered over to anarchy, victimized by every faction, crime increasing, long dissensions rending France. Oh, my God, is this the reward I receive for all my sacrifices? Haven't I tried everything to ensure the happiness of the

French?" And again, during his trial, two officials parrot the fateful words of Caiphas regarding the expediency of one man dying for the people. These were Robespierre, who said, "But Louis must die, because the nation must live." The other, Pierre Manuel, remarked, "One about to die for the good of the world is not to be pitied."

Evident too was the same underlying fear of the people to which the perpetrators in the Gospels were subject, for the good odor of Louis' virtues perfumed the whole scenario, and the people loved him. Like our Lord's, Louis' trial was illegal. As Prudhomme had pointed out to Danton, the Convention had no right to put Louis on trial in the first place: "If the Parliament of England tried Charles I, it is because it was not a Convention. The members of the Conventional Assembly cannot at the same time be accusers, jury and judges." To which Danton enjoined, "You are right, nor shall we judge Louis XVI. We shall kill him!"

Pierre Manuel himself, an ardent revolutionary who helped engineer the famous massacres of August 10 and the following September, was converted and brought to repentance merely by witnessing the King's daily deportment in prison. Three days before the execution he predicted, "If Louis XVI undergoes his sentence, as no doubt he will, the death of Louis XVI will be the death of a saint."

The Procurator Hebert feared the worst: "The Pope will make a new saint of him. Already priests are buying up his remains and making relics of them; already the old women are relaying miracles of this new saint." Hardly a month after the crime even the executioner, Sanson, was moved to write a letter-to-the-editor "in the interests of truth," testifying that the King "bore it all with a composure and fortitude which astonished us. I remain quite convinced that he drew his strength from those religious principles with which no one was more imbued nor more convinced of than he."

Dr. John Moore, an Englishman residing in France during the Revolution, wrote in his journal:

> *The King's appearance in the Convention, the dignified resignation of his manner, the admirable promptitude and candour of his answers, made such an evident impression on some of the audience in the galleries that a determined enemy of Royalty, who had his eye upon them, declared that he was*

afraid of hearing the cry of Vive le Roi! *issue from the tribunes, and added that if the King had remained ten minutes longer in their sight, he was convinced it would have happened: for which reason he was vehemently against his being brought to the bar a second time.*

Even Prudhomme had to admit, "Louis spoke with royal brevity, *brevitate imperatoria*, and all times the Convention's style was cowardly, without force or dignity."

Several apparitions of Louis XVI are said to have occurred, and there have been miracles attributed to his intercession. Our Lord himself is said to have appeared to an Urbanist nun of Fougères to predict the King's death. Two years after the event she testified that He appeared once again and told her:

Rejoice, daughter! I have afflicted you with the death of your King, but I come to console you with this good news: He is in glory, triumphant, and a king in My kingdom. He is crowned, I have given him a scepter and a crown which will be eternal. His scepter and his crown will never be taken from him.

Among the first to voice conviction of the holiness of Louis was the Vicar of Christ. At the secret Consistory called on June 17, 1793, Pius VI stated:

The Most Christian King Louis XVI was condemned to the supreme penalty by an impious conspiracy, and this judgment has been carried out. We shall recall to you in a few words the terms and purposes of this sentence. The National Convention had neither the right nor the authority to pronounce it. In fact, having abolished the monarchy, the best of governments, it transferred all public power to the people, which regulates its conduct neither by reason nor by counsel, forms correct ideas of nothing, appreciates few things according to truth, and evaluates a great number according to popular opinion, which is ever inconstant, easily deceived, drawn to every excess.

Thus reads one of many explicit papal denunciations of modern democracy, which Pius VI compares here unfavorably with monarchy, "the best of governments" most in accord with the natural law laid down by the Creator in the material universe, human society, the family, and man himself.

The most savage part of this people, not satisfied with having degraded the majesty of their King, and determined to wrest his life from him, desired him to be judged by his very accusers, who had declared themselves openly his most implacable enemies. Already from the opening of the trial there were called from the judges in turn some representatives especially noted for their evil dispositions, to make certain that votes for condemnation would prevail among the majority of voices. Even so, the number could not be sufficiently increased to immolate the King on the strength of a legal majority ... We shall pass over in silence here a host of other injustices, nullities and invalidities ... Nor shall We recall everything the King was forced to suffer before being led to the scaffold ...

It is impossible not to be struck with horror by it without repressing all human feeling. Indignation doubles when we consider that this prince's character was universally acknowledged to be gentle and beneficent: that his clemency, his patience, his love for his people never faltered; that incapable of harshness, he always proved himself good-natured and indulgent towards all, and that this excellent natural disposition inspired him with the courage to accede to the public wishes despite all the dangers to his authority and his person that might ensue.

But what above all We cannot pass over in silence is the universal impression of his virtues given by his Testament, written in his own hand, springing from the depth of his soul and published and distributed throughout Europe. What a high opinion do we not form of his virtue! What zeal for the Catholic Faith! What marks of true piety as regards God! What sorrow, what repentance at having set his name despite himself to decrees so contrary to the discipline and orthodox Faith of the Church! Ready to succumb beneath the weight of so much adversity falling ever more heavily on his head day by day, he could say like James I, King of England, that they calumniated him in the assembly of the people, not for having committed a crime, but for being a king, which was regarded as the greatest of crimes.

The most remarkable part of the Allocution follows. Citing the opinion of Pope Benedict XIV, who held that the execution of Mary, Queen of Scots, constituted martyrdom in the true sense of the word, Pius VI asks:

> *Why should we not judge likewise and apply his teaching to the martyrdom of Louis XVI? There is here actually the same attachment to the Faith, the same purpose, the same disastrous end. Therefore there should be like merit. Ah, who could ever doubt that this Monarch was sacrificed principally in hatred for the Faith, and through a spirit of fury against Catholic dogmas?*

Recapitulating the sins of the Enlightenment, the Pope continues:

> *Judging by this uninterrupted flow of impieties originating in France, what man could doubt that it is to hatred for religion that must be imputed the first threads of these plots now troubling and shaking all Europe? No one can deny that the same cause was responsible for the disastrous death of Louis XVI. It is true that they tried to charge this prince with several derelictions of a purely political order. But the principal accusation leveled against him was the unshakable firmness with which he refused to approve or sanction the decree for the deportation of priests, and the letter he wrote to the Bishop of Clermont to let him know that he was entirely resolved to re-establish Catholic worship in France as soon as he could. Isn't all this sufficient to warrant us to believe and maintain without temerity that Louis is a martyr?*

The Holy Father concludes by hoping that:

> *... the immortal blood of Louis may cry out and somehow intercede, that France may realize and abhor her obstinacy in piling so many crimes upon her own head, and may remember the frightful punishments which a just God, Avenger of wrongs, has often inflicted on nations committing assaults of far lesser enormity*

On Pius VI's opinion we may safely rest the case of Louis' martyrdom. In 1942 the theologian Fr. Charton wrote in *The Messenger of the Blessed Virgin*:

> *He was predestined to martyrdom. This alone can unlock the secret of his life and character. Like Jesus his divine Master and Model, he was born a victim. This comparison explains more than the learned theories on the origin and causes of one of the most formidable catastrophes in history ... The ways of human politics are not the ways of God. When God wishes to raise up a martyr - and He is free to do so - what can man find to gainsay? ...*
>
> *Nevertheless, inasmuch as it befits the sovereignty of God to assign to each the destiny awaiting him ... it also befits His goodness to fashion each heart for the role it is destined to fill ... It is in the light of this divine vocation and heroic submission that we must place ourselves if we wish to judge the life of the Martyr-King from a Christian point of view, the only true one. A martyred king he is, and he is nothing other ... By an effect of the gift of the Holy Ghost which is the gift of understanding, he wanted to save France the way he had to save her, in other words, the way Christ saved the world ... In the person of her King, France herself died as did Christ. And that is why she is immortal!*

Viewing Louis in this light, we are not surprised to learn that he was passionately devoted to the Sacred Heart of Jesus, whose adoration was preached to the French royal family by St. John Eudes even before the revelations destined for his great-grandfather Louis XIV had been made to St. Margaret Mary. According to Mgr. Delassus, "He had turned his prison cell into a veritable oratory, whereas Most Christian King he lived a holy life with his family, all of them offering the homage of their lives morning and evening." All wore the emblem of the Sacred Heart, to Whom beautiful prayers were composed by the Queen and her sister-in-law Madame Elisabeth, both of whom would in due time follow Louis to the guillotine.

A consecration signed by them has come down to us which reads:

> *O Jesus Christ, in charity we gather every heart in this kingdom, from the heart of our august monarch to that of the poorest of his subjects, to offer all to you. Yes, Heart of Jesus, we offer you our whole nation and the hearts of all her children ... O Holy Virgin, they are in your hands. We have drawn them together by consecrating ourselves to you as our mother and protectress. This day we beg you, offer them to the Heart of Jesus. Proffered by you He will accept them. He will forgive them. He will bless them. He will sanctify, He will save France totally and revive holy religion in her.*

From the royal prison devotion to the Sacred Heart was renewed throughout the nation, the badge becoming the official insignia of the heroic popular resistance in the Vendee and elsewhere. Worn to the last by countless other martyrs in all ranks of society, it remained as a pledge among the general population, the vast majority of whom never desired their Revolution any more than most American colonials wanted theirs, and who received the news of their sovereign's death with grief and consternation.

In 1909 Pope St. Pius X in an interview with the French Foreign Minister Emile Flourens, said, "Believe me, I know your French people. They are Catholic and monarchist by nature. Sooner or later they'll come back!" According to the Marquis de la Franquerie, Padre Pio is said to have told his confidant:

> *The true greatness of France lies in the royal power of David which resided in the land of France, in the blood of King Louis and Marie Antoinette, victims who died for Christ through the brutality of the beast, the satanic revolution. Because of King Louis' forgiveness, and to recognize in the king the power of divine love ... In the silence of prayer God will choose His elect for the good of France and the world.*

It is said that shortly before Louis XVI's incarceration, with the help of Fr. Hebert, Father General of the Eudists and likewise a victim of the Revolution (not to be confused with the Procurator Hebert), the king drafted a "Vow to the Sacred Heart," promising to consecrate France to the Sacred of Heart as requested a century before through St. Margaret Mary. Because the Vow was discovered sealed in a wall years after the King's death, some doubt has been cast on its authenticity, but it has continued to nourish the hopes of many a devout royalist to this day.

Such a pledge on the part of the last properly anointed head of Christendom could not fail to arouse the satanic forces laboring to destroy the last vestiges of Christianity. Is it genuine? We may believe so if we give credence to the appearance of the Sacred Heart to Sr. Lucy of Fatima. When speaking of the delay of the Pope and the bishops in making the Consecration of Russia to the Immaculate Heart of Mary, He promised her, "Like the King of France, they will repent and do so, but it will be late."

Heaven and earth await the accomplishment of these two Consecrations to the Hearts of Jesus and Mary, one of France, the other of Russia, on which God is pleased to hang the peace of the world. Not until one and the other are complied with, can Church and state be reunited and human society healed. That this will happen infallibly, we must believe in the face of hell, for Our Lord told St. Margaret Mary that He would reign in spite of Satan and all opposition. And at Fatima Our Lady promised that her Immaculate Heart would triumph.

IMMORTAL BLOOD OF LOUIS, CRY OUT AND HASTEN
THE DAY!

POSTSCRIPT

Because Sacred Scripture relates true history, the Christmas story does not tell us that Christ was born, but that He is born. God, whose very name is *I Am*, forever begets His Son "this day" through the Holy Ghost in Bethlehem, in the bosom of the Blessed Trinity, in the womb of the Immaculate Virgin Mary, and in the hearts of men.

History is not just a chronological record of events. Its proper function is prophetic, to show the past and the future in the present. The more we study history, the more we see that, apart from the present, past and future can hardly be said to exist at all. They solicit our attention only by virtue of that mysterious component of material creation we call time. Apart from time, past and future would be reduced to a constant present, and the drama of mankind would unfold very differently, like that of the angels.

Eternity, revelation tells us, is precisely an everlasting present, without past or future. There is order in heaven, but things do not happen there in succession as they do on earth. There will be an end of time because it is temporary. It is only the means whereby eternity is converted into successive fragments apprehendable to our senses in this life. For the time being, we might say, time makes eternity temporal. To some degree, what happens is analogous to the way God became man, so we could know Him here below, through our senses. We might go so far as to say that time is the incarnation of eternity.

If the past seems always to be receding from view into the mists of antiquity, that is due to our defective perception, which can deal only piecemeal with reality. The same is true of the future, which is already whole and entire in the present, if we could only see it. Folk wisdom tells us, "The past is prologue," or "Whoever will not learn from the past is doomed to repeat it," but Scripture tells us, "Nothing under the sun is new. . What is it that hath been done? The same shall be done"(*Eccles. 1:10,9*). Exposing the past automatically unlocks the future, for in the present all three are one. This is a reflection of the trinitarian mystery in the very heart of reality. If history is to serve any practical purpose, it is essential to keep all this in mind.

In this life our only point of contact with eternity is that moment of time we call the present. It is our only access to reality. As that great director of souls Father de Caussade taught, only by seizing "the grace of the present moment" can we conform our wills to reality and save our souls. Nothing whatever happens in the past or in the future. It is only in the present, at that point where time and eternity converge, that history is made. By our free acts we all make history, whether we like it or not. History is the sum of the free acts of intelligent beings.

St. Francis de Sales said, "Each moment comes to us bearing an order from God, and it will implant itself in eternity, to remain forever what we will have made of it." The consequence is either salvation or damnation. That is what history is all about. In fact, if mankind's ultimate destiny is not kept in mind, history makes no sense at all. History will never explain the mystery of Predestination, but properly read *sub specie aeternitatis*, in the light of eternity, it can show how this most difficult of Catholic dogmas is in no way contrary to reason.

The ability to discern the past and the future in the present pertains to the gift called prophecy, a talent not normal to fallen human nature, but one which God in His mercy occasionally bestows on certain individuals during crucial periods for the good of all. Barring this extraordinary gift, it is supernatural faith, working through reason, which is our ordinary means of seeing the past and future events of history in the present. The key to understanding history therefore does not lie primarily in research, but in the deepening of the prayer life and in union with God.

St. Bernard says in one of his Christmas sermons, "Faith may be regarded as an image of eternity, comprehending as it does, in its most ample bosom, all things past, present and to come, so that nothing escapes it, nothing is lost to it, nothing lies beyond its range." Donoso Cortes called theology the light of history, because it alone can apply faith systematically to events, enabling us to see past, present and future as one whole in their eternal aspect and to decipher their meaning.

"Blessed are they that have not seen and have believed" (*John 20:29*). In our blindness, due to original sin, we must believe what God tells us about our past and our future in order to be able to deal with the present, because outside faith there is only ignorance and uncertainty. Although unaided reason often leads us to suspect the truth in any given case, there is no way of verifying it, and error becomes the rule. To make any sense history must therefore be approached metaphysically, from a standpoint beyond itself and the world it describes.

Without reference to the bedrock certainties of revelation, history is at best an interminable roster of unrelated, chaotic incidents which just "happen" and which lend themselves to any desired interpretation. Morality has no place in scenarios where free will plays no part, where events are the automatic outcome of blind chance and conflicting interests. In this kind of history nothing really happens at all, for it has already taken place.

Real history, such as we find in the Christmas story, always takes its position in God's eternal Now. In the Apocalypse God reveals to mankind events which presumably have not yet happened and which are still to come, yet it never leaves the present. The Lord who is born at Bethlehem orders St. John to "write therefore the things which thou hast seen, and which are, and which must be done hereafter" (*Apo. 1:19*), for all are one. Seven times He predicts His second coming, and each time it is in the present tense: "Behold, I come quickly!" That is history.

SELECTED BIBLIOGRAPHY

Agreda, Ven. Maria de Jésus, *Mistica Ciudad de Dios*

J Ahern, Patrick H., *The Life of John J. Keane*

Arrninjon, Fr. Charles-Marie Antoine, *The End of the Present World*

Bainvel, S.J., Fr. J., *Devotion to the Sacred Heart*

Barrows, J.H., ed. *The World's Parliament of Religions*

Boucher and Tehan, *Prince of Democracy: James Cardinal Gibbons*

Brinton, Crane, *Anatomy of Revolution*

Brooke, Tal, *When the World Will Be as One*

Buathier, Fr. J. M., *Le Sacrifice dans le Dogme Catholique*

Condorcet, Marquis Marie-Jean Antoine, *Influencia de la Revoluccion de America sobre Europa*

Cross, Robert D., *The Emergence of Liberal Catholicism in America*

de la Franquerie, Marquis André, *Ascendances Davidiques des Rois de France; Jeanne d'Arc la Pucelle; Le Caractère Sacré et Divin de la Royauté en France; Le Sacré Couer et la France; Louis XVI le Roi Martyr.*

De Maistre, Joseph, *Considerations on France; The Generative Power of Political Constitutions; The Pope*

de Coursac, Girault, *Louis XVI Roi Martyr*

Delassus, Mgr. Henri, *La Mission Posthume de Sainte Jeanne d'Arc*

de Poncins, Leon, *Judaism and the Vatican*

des Mousseaux, Gougenot, *Le Juif*

Disraeli, Benjamin, *Coningsby*

Donoso Cortes, Don Juan, *Catholicism, Liberalism and Socialism*

Dupont, Yves, *More about the Great Monarch*

Ellis, Fr. John Tracey, *American Catholicism*

Ferchaud, Claire, *Notes Autobiographiques*

Gonthier, J., *Malédictions et Bénédictions*

Hall, Manly Palmer, *The Secret Destiny of America*

Hanson, J.W., *World Parliament of Religions*

Ireland, Archbishop John, *The Church and Modem Society*

Journet, Charles, *The Church and the Word Incarnate*

Judant, Denise, *Jalons pour une Théologie Chrétienne d'Israël*

Lazare, Bernard, *L 'Antisémitisme*

Lernann, Fr. Joseph, *Les Juifs dans la Revolution Francoise; Napoleon et les Juifs*

Lilienthal, Alfred, *Zionist Connection II*

Nock, Albert J., *The Theory of Education in the United States*

Pernoud, Regine, *The Retrial of Joan of Arc*

Pike, Albert, *Morals and Dogma*

Pius X, *Our Apostolic Mandate*

Quigley, Carroll, *Tragedy and Hope*

Rager, Fr. John, *The Political Philosophy of Bl. Cardinal Bellarmine*

Ruderman, Jerome, *Jews in American History*

Sackville-West, Victoria, *Saint Joan of Arc*

Savage, Minot J., *World's Congress of Religions*

Soloviev, Vladimir, *The Universal Church*

Virion, Pierre, *Le Mystere de Jeanne d'Arc et la Politique des Nations*

Zaratti, Fr. Alfonso, *The Work of the Catholic Church in the United States*

ABOUT THE AUTHOR

An established writer before the Second Vatican Council, Solange Hertz wrote for most major Catholic periodicals and had five books to her credit, one a selection of the Catholic Literary Foundation. When she refused to adjust her theology to the new "Spirit of Vatican II," her manuscripts almost overnight became unacceptable to her former editors. After a series of articles on feminine spirituality for the old *Triumph* magazine, she continued speaking for tradition by successfully producing on her own, *The Thought of His Heart*, and *Sin Revisited*.

In 1973 she began writing the *Big Rock Papers*, published privately throughout the next decade and the source of the highly acclaimed *Star Spangled Heresy: Americanism*, published in 1992. Currently her articles can be found in *The Remnant*, and abroad in *Apropos*, *Christian Order* and *Action Familiale et Scolaire*. Mrs. Hertz is universally regarded as one of traditional Catholicism's foremost contemporary writers and lecturers.